DAYS OF JUBILEE

The End of Slavery in the United States

Patricia C. &
Fredrick L. McKissack

SCHOLASTIC PRESS
NEW YORK

Copyright © 2003 by Patricia C. and Fredrick L. McKissack
All rights reserved. Published by Scholastic Press, a division of Scholastic Inc., *Publishers since 1920.*
SCHOLASTIC, SCHOLASTIC PRESS, and associated logos are trademarks and/or registered trademarks of
Scholastic Inc. No part of this publication may be reproduced, or stored in a retrieval system, or
transmitted in any form or by any means, electronic, mechanical, photocopying, recording, or
otherwise, without written permission of the publisher. For information regarding permission,
write to Scholastic Inc., Attention: Permissions Department, 557 Broadway, New York, NY 10012.

LIBRARY OF CONGRESS CATALOGING-IN-PUBLICATION DATA

Days of Jubilee: the end of slavery in the United States / by Patricia C. and Fredrick L. McKissack.
p.   cm.   Summary: Uses slave narratives, letters, diaries, military orders, and other documents to chronicle
the various stages leading to the emancipation of slaves in the United States.
ISBN 0-590-10764-X

1. Slaves — Emancipation — United States — Juvenile literature. 2. Slaves — Emancipation — United
States — Sources — Juvenile literature. 3. African Americans — History — To 1863 — Juvenile literature.
4. African Americans — History — To 1863 — Sources — Juvenile literature. 5. United States History —
Civil War, 1861–1863 — Juvenile literature. 6. United States — History — Civil War, 1861–1863
Sources — Juvenile literature. [1. Slaves — Emancipation. 2. African Americans — History — To 1863.
3. United States — History — Civil War, 1861–1863 — Sources.] I. McKissack, Frederick. II. Title.
E453.M28 2002   973.7 — dc21   2001057568

3   4   5   6   7   8   9   10   04   05   06   07

First edition, February 2003
Book design by David Caplan
Printed in the United States of America
The text type was set in 13-pt. AGaramond.

For

Sarilda Blake,

Yvonne and Tom Rocco,

Nancy Sheridan,

Connie and George Stephans,

Doris and Bob Becker,

Becky and Grant Nelson,

and Jo and Dave Dean —

good neighbors and good friends

CONTENTS

———◦—◦(◦)◦—◦———

WHEN HALLELUJAH
BROKE OUT

⸻ ⊶◉⊷ ⸻

THIS BOOK IS TITLED *DAYS OF JUBILEE* because there wasn't one day when all the slaves were freed at the same time. It was much more personal than that. Whenever slaves learned they were free, that day became *their* Jubilee and that's the day they remembered and cared about. Slaves weren't concerned with documents and proclamations. They responded to real and present results. If a general told them they were free, then the general was their deliverer. When they heard that President Lincoln had set *some* slaves free, then they counted themselves in that number and headed for Washington where the Great Emancipator lived. It was an uncomplicated understanding of freedom, one they could easily grasp.

We have relied upon slave narratives as our primary source of information in telling this story. The narratives were collected by writers during the 1930s and are housed in the Library of Congress in Washington, D.C. Although there is no one day on which all former slaves celebrated, such as the Fourth of July, Thanksgiving Day, or Labor Day, black people were united in the oneness of their desire to be free. Dates, times, and places were unimportant.

Whenever and wherever freedom came, they celebrated in the moment in their hearts and minds.

African slavery came to the New World with Christopher Columbus, and it took almost 373 years and a terrible war to be rid of it in the United States. The full scope of what their ancestors had endured was not within the grasp of the slave in the antebellum South. They could only measure their long suffering by their own experiences. But the souls of all those slaves who survived the Middle Passage — many thousands gone — must have felt some vindication when freedom came.

For the millions who'd faced the slave block, who'd acquiesced to survive, who'd led rebellions and died fighting, who'd run away, or who'd toiled all their lives in captivity — for them, the ending of slavery in the United States was a time of unequaled happiness. It was a time to pray, praise, and give thanks, and they celebrated. As one slave described it: "The end of the war, it come just like that — like you snap your fingers . . . How did we know it? Hallelujah broke out! Folks was singing and shouting all over."

This is a story about real events and people. Whenever possible we have let them speak for themselves. Now come rejoice with us as we tell you the story of how an oppressed people celebrated their various days of Jubilee.

PATRICIA C. & FREDRICK L. McKISSACK
Chesterfield, Missouri

DAYS
OF
JUBILEE

ROAD TO JUBILEE GOT MANY TWISTS AND TURNS

—————◦((◦))◦—————

"For Mas' and his family, the Fourth Day [of July] was their Jubilee. That's when they all got free to be. Mas' give us the day off to celebrate 'long with them. And we did. But all the time we was wishin' for our own day of independence."

WILLIAM COLE
Lebanon, Tennessee
Slave Narrative

JULY 8, 1776

It is hot and humid in Philadelphia. Beads of perspiration have formed on the brow of James Forten, an affluent gentleman of color who has made his fortune as a sailmaker and businessman. Unaccustomed to being shoved and pushed by a potentially unruly crowd, Forten holds his position, refusing to give up his spot in front of the statehouse door. He has come to hear the reading of the Declaration of Independence, which members of the Continental Congress signed four days earlier.

Taking in the scene, Forten looks up at the bell tower. The inscription on the bell is: PROCLAIM LIBERTY THROUGHOUT THE LAND UNTO ALL THE INHABITANTS THEREOF. *Forten smiles as he dabs at his face with a handkerchief. He has never felt that the king's words applied to him — a man of African descent. Will this new declaration include him now? That is why he has come.*

At last, the nation's birth certificate is read. And James Forten gulps in the ideas like a thirsty man. Others around him are ignited by the powerful and moving words. "We hold these truths to be self-evident, that all men are created equal . . ." And in their joy, people hurry to ring the Bell of Liberty. Then they rip down the king's coat of arms and burn it.

Forten goes home filled with joy but his soul is calm and at peace. Jefferson's lofty words have finally confirmed what Forten knows to be true: All men are created equal and are endowed by their Creator with "certain unalienable Rights" such as "Life, Liberty, and the pursuit of Happiness." For Forten this is a day of Jubilee. He celebrates by joining the Continental army, secure in the knowledge that no country founded on the principles of equality would continue to tolerate slavery and injustice.

During the colonial period, African slaves were often freed after honorably serving in the various militias and wars. Of the 300,000 men who fought in the Revolutionary War, 5,000 had been blacks, many of them freed after service. Both freedmen of color and slaves fought side by side with their white counterparts to win for themselves and their families those rights and privileges that had been stated clearly in the Declaration of Independence. They truly believed that those ideals would apply to them if they showed themselves worthy.

Yet most of the black Revolutionary War veterans in the South were returned to slavery. Those who were freed either stayed in the South under restrictive conditions or migrated north. In both regions they formed thriving African American communities — in Charleston as well as New York, in Baltimore as well as Philadelphia and Boston. Some free Southern blacks became skilled craftsmen and farmers and even owned slaves of their own. But free blacks in the South were far outnumbered by their Northern counterparts. Fugitive slaves, such as Frederick Douglass, Sojourner Truth, Harriet Tubman, and others fled north and joined whites who formed the core of the ever-growing antislavery movement.

James Forten was an important abolitionist. His voice was strong and consistently against slavery and when it came to African American civil liberties, he was usually at the forefront, investing time, energy, and his wealth to the cause. For Forten and other free black men of his generation, the Fourth of July was consid-

James Forten, prominent Philadelphia businessman, abolitionist, and black leader. (The Historical Society of Pennsylvania)

ered their day of Jubilee. That is why he was shocked and dismayed when the United States Constitution was ratified without abolishing slavery. In fact, several clauses legalized it, and made it necessary to pass a constitutional amendment to abolish U.S. slavery. Then the first ten amendments — the Bill of Rights — were drafted, and still, slavery was not ended.

Fifty years after James Forten had declared the Fourth of July a day of Jubilee, he was told that a mob had driven away black citizens who'd come to Liberty Hall in Philadelphia to take part in the July Fourth festivities. Outraged, Forten spoke forcefully against the injustice, saying sarcastically, "It is a well-known fact that black people upon certain days of publick jubilee, dare not be seen after twelve o'clock in the day. I allude particularly to the Fourth of July — Is it not wonderful that the day set apart for the festival of Liberty should be abused by the advocates of freedom, in endeavoring to [soil or spoil?] what they profess to adore?"

Years later, in 1852, another African American leader, Frederick Douglass, was asked by the Rochester [New York] Ladies' Anti-Slavery Society to make a Fourth of July speech. He agreed but insisted upon making the speech on the

A former slave, Frederick Douglass became a leading spokesperson for the abolition of slavery and for racial equality. (National Portrait Gallery, Smithsonian Institution, Washington, D.C.)

fifth rather than the fourth. In one of his best-known public address-es, Douglass strongly protested the lack of freedom and justice in America, reminding the audience ". . . the Fourth of July is yours, not mine . . . You citizens mock me by asking me to speak today?"

African Americans did not view the Fourth of July as a day to celebrate freedom until after the Civil War. Instead, they celebrat-ed the fifth of July as a form of protest.

For a while some African Americans embraced January 1 as a day of liberation or one they hoped would lead to the total eman-cipation of slaves. A bill signed by Thomas Jefferson on January 1, 1808, supposedly put an end to the transatlantic slave trade. Reverend Absalom Jones, a leader in the Free African Society of Philadelphia and a well-known member of the Episcopal clergy, felt certain that the bill would lead to the end of slavery in America. This belief led Reverend Jones to pronounce:

"Let the first of January . . . be set apart in every year, as a day of publick thanksgiving. Let the history of the sufferings of our brethren, and of their deliverance, descend by this means to our children, to the remotest generations; and when they shall ask, in time to come, saying, What mean the lessons, the psalms, the prayers and the praises in the worship of this day? let us answer them by saying, the Lord, on the day of which this is the anniversary, abolished the trade which dragged your fathers from their native country, and sold them as bond men in the United States of America."

Jones and other men of his day, such as Reverend Richard Allen and James Forten, believed that the practice of slavery would end by lack of necessity. They did not live to see the end of the system because the invention of the cotton gin made the production of cotton profitable. The demand for slaves increased to maintain the enormous labor needs. Though it was illegal to transport slaves from Africa to the United States, it was still legal to buy and sell slaves from the Caribbean and Brazil. There was no law against the practice of "breeding" slaves like cattle or sheep within the United States.

And though the United States Constitution ended the transatlantic slave trade, trafficking in African captives continued until after the Civil War. But the people in bondage never wavered in their hope that one day Jubilee would come.

The Clothilde, *a slave ship with 130 men, women, and children who had been stolen from a Tarkbar village in West Africa, docked in Mobile Harbor at night on July 9, 1859. The ship's captain, William Fowler, eluded federal boats patrolling the Mississippi Sound, unloaded the ship, and burned it. Fowler couldn't sell the slaves, so when the Civil War began, he set the captives free. Under the leadership of Cudjoe Lewis, the Africans were able to stay together and formed a village called Africa Town in an area known as the Plateau, near Mobile. Here they celebrated their Jubilee before the emancipation of their fellow slaves. They were able to keep their African names and customs. Descendants of these last African captives can still be found in east Mobile. Cudjoe Lewis, the last of the original Tarkbar villagers, died in 1935.*

FREEDOM A-COMIN', ANYHOW

———◦◦◉◦◦———

"A geographical line has been drawn across the Union, and all the states north of that line have united in the election of a man to the high office of President of the United States whose opinions and purposes are hostile to Slavery. He is to be entrusted with the administration of the common Government, because he has declared that 'Government cannot endure permanently half slave, half free,' and that the public mind must rest in the belief that Slavery is in the course of ultimate extinction."

SOUTH CAROLINA'S DECLARATION OF CAUSES OF SECESSION

December 4, 1860

NOVEMBER 8, 1860

En route to Florida

Mary Chesnut, wife of Senator James Chesnut, Jr., from South Carolina, is traveling to Fernandina, Florida, with her thirteen-year-old companion, Tanny Withers. The train has stopped to allow passengers to disembark and to take on new passengers. Suddenly, a woman shouts, "That settles the hash!" Mary notices that boarding travelers appear shocked, dismayed; others look more hurt and disappointed. She sends Tanny to find out what is going on.

Reporting on what is the matter, Tanny touches Mary on the shoulder and whispers with disgust, "Lincoln's been elected!" His young eyes express the disbelief Mary is feeling. "They've really done it. Elected Abraham Lincoln," the boy says angrily.

"Wait!" Mary tries to ease the tension that's mounting inside her. "We need to be absolutely sure before we become too alarmed."

"That man over there has a telegram," Tanny answers, pointing toward a gentleman whose face is twisted in a scowl.

Soon everyone is talking at the same time — each voice growing louder and more excited than the next. One elderly man, obviously moved by the news, shakes his head despondently: "The die is cast; no more vain regrets; sad forebodings are useless; the stake is life or death."

Mary hears another person call out bitterly, "Now that the black radical Republicans have the power I suppose they will brown us all." It is easy to get caught up in the drama of the moment, especially when someone proclaims prematurely, "South Carolina has seceded."

Mary knows that South Carolina has not seceded, but she hopes her state will leave the Union and that other Southern states will follow. Mary decides at that moment to record her feelings on this day and others to follow. She will keep a journal, to tell the story in her own voice. She will write later, "I write so that . . . when this thing is finally over there will be some record of what happened" from the Southern woman's point of view.

The Civil War diaries of Mary Chestnut and other Southern women provide a window through which each new generation can observe attitudes, actions, and motives that were the foundation of the Confederacy. When Chesnut began keeping her diary in 1860 she was forty years old and childless. Married to James Chesnut, a United States senator from South Carolina before secession and later an

Mary Chesnut's Civil War diaries became principal source materials for her famous portrait of the Confederacy. (Private Collection/Art Resource, NY)

officer in the Confederate army, she was a member of the Southern elite and a slaveholder. She enjoyed the social life of Washington and, by all accounts, was a well-informed, intelligent, and articulate woman — slightly ahead of her time.

As a Southern senator's wife, Chesnut had watched with interest as the political bantering over slavery had become more and more strident and divisive since 1850. The critical issue was not about the abolition of slavery, but whether slavery should be permitted to spread beyond the region into the western territories.

The Missouri Compromise of 1820 had established the Mason-Dixon Line, which permitted states to enter as slave or free depending upon their location above or below this imaginary line.

The Kansas-Nebraska Act of 1854 allowed territories to determine whether slavery would be legal within their borders, which made it a state's rights issue. This legislation set off heated debates that eventually led to violence.

In 1856 the first Republican National Convention was held and Senator John C. Frémont was nominated for president of the United States. Running on the slogan, "Free soil, free labor, free speech and free men." Frémont, in a three-way race, was able to win one third of the popular vote. But the Democrat James Buchanan was elected.

During Buchanan's administration, the U.S. Supreme Court ruled in the Dred Scott case that "blacks had no rights that white men were bound to honor" and also that the Missouri Compromise was unconstitutional. This was a serious blow to the antislavery movement.

Meanwhile, Republicans worked harder to gain seats in Congress to block legislation that would allow slavery in the western territories. By 1858 the Republicans had taken control of the House of Representatives, and in 1859 the whole South was shocked when John Brown led a raid on Harper's Ferry, Virginia (now West Virginia), with the purpose of seizing arms and leading an armed rebellion among the slaves. Although he was captured and hanged, Brown became a hero of the abolitionist cause.

As the political climate heated up, Chesnut and her Southern neighbors were particularly troubled by the political rise of an Illinois lawyer named Abraham Lincoln, an articulate spokesman for the Republicans. On May 16, 1860, when Abraham Lincoln was nominated for president on the Republican ticket, South Carolinians began to speak of secession.

But Lincoln was not an abolitionist. Though he believed slavery was wrong, he campaigned on the platform that he had no intention of interfering with slavery in the states where it existed. He said he thought he didn't have the authority to do so as the president who had to pledge an oath to uphold and defend the Constitution.

Although the word *slavery* is not used in the Constitution, the fugitive slave clause protects slaveholders' "property rights" and legalizes the institution. To abolish slavery it would take a constitutional amendment ratified by the states, and that wasn't likely to happen in 1860.

Though Mary Chesnut occasionally expressed doubts about

slavery, she remained convinced that African people were no more than "a horde of idle dirty beasts." The election of Abraham Lincoln and the possible emancipation of four million black men, women, and children threatened the well-ordered world of the Chesnuts and the slaveholding governing class.

The South Carolina congressional delegation promised to secede if Lincoln won. Abraham Lincoln was elected president in

Abraham Lincoln.
(Library of Congress)

the November election of 1860, and South Carolina made good on its promise. On December 4, 1860, South Carolina became the first state to secede from the Union.

Congress tried in vain to persuade the South not to take such drastic measures. Senator John J. Crittenden of Kentucky introduced a resolution stating unequivocally that the government had no intention of "overthrowing or interfering with the rights or established institutions of the seceded states." He hoped that it might appease South Carolina. It didn't.

Mrs. Eugene McLean, another Civil War diarist, was married to a Union officer from Maryland. She remembered seeing Senator John Crittenden in Congress:

"Mr. Crittenden [of Kentucky] spoke today in a trembling voice and with tearful eyes, beseeching those who could save the Union. I could not control my feelings; it was sad to see that old white-haired man, who had devoted his best years to his country, find himself powerless to help it in this its extremity, but, with piteous entreaties to deaf ears and hardened hearts, exhaust himself in the vain effort to bring about a single concession . . ."

Slave quarters, Preservation Plantation, South Carolina. (New-York Historical Society)

Meanwhile, in the quarters, where the slaves lived, they knew something big was about to happen. They pieced the story together from overheard conversations, print material found in the trash and read by secret readers, and whispered words. Since 99 percent of the slaves were illiterate, the threads that bound them together were primarily oral. Word-of-mouth transmissions traveled like the echoes of African drums, with successive recipients picking up the relay and passing it on. They couldn't know all the details — some never knew what the war was really about — but they knew the conflict between whites offered an opportunity for them to emancipate themselves. After 1860, escapes increased and the Underground Railroad became more active than ever. "Folk commenced to getting happy," remembered a former slave. "If their masters were so frightened by President Lincoln, then he must be the long-awaited Moses" who would usher in the day of Jubilee.

While the slaves waited, they sang songs about what they would do when they were freed. Heaven was the slaves' metaphor for freedom.

> I got shoes.
> You got shoes.
> All of God's chullin' got shoes.
> When I get to heaven
> Gon' put on my shoes
> And gon' walk all over God's heaven.

◆ ◆ ◆

The idea of freedom emboldened some slaves, who decided to *take* their freedom instead of waiting for someone to bring it to them. In a parish outside New Orleans, a slave named Mosley planned a rebellion for March 4, 1861, the same day that President Lincoln gave his first inaugural speech. It failed. When Mosley was captured, he said what most of his people believed, and what their masters feared was true: "Lincoln will set us free."

But Mosley's hopes were not to be realized as quickly as the slaves or their masters might have expected. During his first inaugural speech President Lincoln extended an olive branch to the rebellious states — even though six other states had seceded by March — saying, "We must not be enemies." He reassured the South that he had no plans to end slavery. In fact, he supported a proposed Constitutional amendment, "to the effect that the Federal Government shall never interfere with the domestic institutions of the States, including that of persons held to service . . . I have no objection to its being made express and irrevocable."

While the president was willing to compromise on the issue of slavery at this point, he would not on secession. He warned the rebels that all seceded states were still in the Union and subject to federal law. And though he wanted to avoid a war, President Lincoln was firmly committed to preserving the Union, using whatever means necessary.

Words. More words. Southern leaders ignored them all. In February, rebel leaders had met in Alabama, to form the

Confederate States of America and write a constitution. It resembled the United States Constitution, but there were substantial changes made to protect slavery.

Alexander Stephens, who later became vice president of the Confederacy, told a crowd in Savannah, Georgia: "Our new Government is founded . . . upon the great truth that the Negro is not equal to the white man; that slavery, subordination to the superior race, is his natural and moral condition. This, our new Government, is the first, in the history of the world, based upon this great physical, philosophical, and moral truth."

Attitudes would eventually change on both sides, but in early 1861, Lincoln's policy was to preserve the Union even if it meant tolerating slavery. The Confederacy's goal was to guarantee states' rights and the continuation of the slave system, even if it meant disunion.

BE BACK 'FORE BREAKFAST

—◦◉◦—

"When the war come on, the old man Hawkens was dead. The widow Hawkens had three sons. One son went to the war, but he didn't want to go. He asked his mother if she'd rather free the Negroes or go to war. She said, 'Go fight . . . you'll be home for breakfast.'"

Slave Narrative

1861

Nicholas Biddle is a sixty-five-year-old fugitive slave who makes his living in Pottsville, Pennsylvania, selling beverages in the summer and oysters in the winter. Two days after President Lincoln's call to arms, he attaches himself in an unenlisted capacity to a company under the command of Captain James Curtin. His goal is to bring freedom to those who are still living in bondage.

Now he is on his way to Washington to take a stand. The company passes through Harrisburg. There, blacks are delighted to see one of their own in uniform going "to strike a blow for freedom." They wave white handkerchiefs and shout joyfully when they see Biddle.

When the troops stop for the night, several whites are curious about Biddle. One soldier says playfully, "Did you ever think that if a rebel catches you, you might be taken to Georgia and sold?" to which Biddle answers, "I go to Washington, a-trustin' in the Lord, and the devil himself and the other Plug-Uglies [rebels] can't scare me. You the one better look out."

Arriving in Baltimore, Maryland, at noon on April 18, 1861, the troops prepare to go from one railroad station to another. Seeing Biddle among the white soldiers causes an unruly mob to gather. Unlike the shouts of praise and joy in Harrisburg, now there are jeers and curses. Biddle continues to march, looking straight ahead. The mob throws things and swears at all the white soldiers, "Welcome to a Southern grave, N—— Lovers."

Suddenly Biddle is struck in the face. "Kill that b—— brother of Abraham Lincoln." Biddle staggers and almost falls, but an officer supports him. Other troops hurry to the train station, protecting Biddle against the mob as they go. Surely the mob will do Biddle harm if they get their hands on him. The troops — with Biddle among them — arrive in Washington in the early evening.

Days later there is a full-scale riot in Baltimore against the 6th Regiment of the Massachusetts Volunteers, resulting in the death of four soldiers and six civilians.

> *What happens to Biddle after this is unknown, but his friends place the following inscription on his tombstone:*
>
> HIS WAS THE PROUD DISTINCTION OF SHEDDING THE FIRST BLOOD IN THE LATER WAR FOR THE UNION, BEING WOUNDED WHILE MARCHING THROUGH BALTIMORE WITH THE FIRST VOLUNTEERS FROM SCHUYLKILL COUNTY, 18 APRIL, 1861.

Fort Sumter unarmed.

Waiting like a sitting duck.

Rebel cannons blast.

The South viewed Fort Sumter, located in Charleston Harbor, as the property of a foreign power on Southern soil. Major Robert Anderson, commander of the fort, notified President Lincoln that he needed to be resupplied. Lincoln knew that if he sent a ship it might be misunderstood as an act of war. If he failed to service the fort, then he wouldn't be fulfilling his responsibility as commander in chief of the military. Lincoln decided to inform Jefferson Davis that an unarmed supply ship would relieve the soldiers and their families who were housed at Fort Sumter. The next move was up to President Davis.

Davis and other Southern leaders felt Lincoln's action was an affront to the Confederacy and responded by ordering the attack on federally occupied Fort Sumter at 4:30 A.M., April 12, 1861. Thirty-three hours later, the Union commander, having no casualties but lacking supplies, surrendered. One person was killed accidentally afterward.

Texas, Arkansas, Tennessee, and Virginia had joined the Confederacy by May 1861, and North Carolina was the last state to secede. Missouri, Maryland, Kentucky, and Delaware were slave states that remained loyal to the Union.

On the day that Fort Sumter was captured by the Confederates, President Lincoln drew up a proclamation calling for 75,000 Northern volunteers to build up the standing Union army, which stood at only 16,367 officers and soldiers. The response was over-

Soldiers of the First New York Engineers at Fort Sumter. (Massachusetts Historical Society)

whelming. Whites enlisted in record numbers. By the late spring of 1861, volunteers from all over New England had been called to Washington, because President Lincoln wanted to end the rebellion by capturing Richmond, the Confederate capital.

> *"Nobody hurt, after all. How gay we were last night. Reaction after the dread of all the slaughter we thought those dreadful cannons were making such a noise in doing.*
>
> *Fort Sumter has been on fire. He has not yet silenced any of our guns. So the aides — still with swords and red sashes by way of uniform — tell us."*
>
> MARY CHESNUT, *April 13, 1861*

From city to city, state to state, African American men — like Nicholas Biddle — wanted to enlist. "Let us strike a blow for freedom!" For them, however, the war wasn't just about preserving the Union. Free blacks were committed to a nation free of slavery and they wanted to fight for that end. But the secretary of war issued an order stating that "this Department has no intention to call into the service any colored soldiers."

In September 1861, Frederick Douglass wrote an editorial accusing Lincoln of trying to fight the Confederates with one hand tied behind his back. "No war but an Abolition war; no peace but an Abolition peace; liberty for all, chains for none . . ."

It might have been "policy" not to enlist blacks in the military, but that didn't stop them from serving in other capacities, such as cooks, porters, and laborers. Some commanding officers ignored the policy and allowed blacks to join their ranks. Blacks were willing to do anything to help strike a blow for freedom and bring the day of Jubilee a little closer to reality.

The stage was set. The players were on mark. But nobody knew the drama that would unfold over the next four years. Few on either side thought the war would last as long as it did or that the death

Jefferson Davis, president of the Confederacy, with his wife. (Library of Congress)

toll would be so high. Jefferson Davis, convinced that it was going to be a bloodless revolution, made the unfortunate vow at LaGrange, Mississippi, that he would drink all the blood spilled by Confederate soldiers during the conflict.

In preparing to respond to the bombing of Fort Sumter, President Lincoln appointed General Irvin McDowell as the commanding general of the Union forces. McDowell warned Lincoln that his soldiers were not ready to engage in battle. They were young, inexperienced, undisciplined, and untrained. But Lincoln argued that the Confederates were just as green and ordered McDowell to advance.

On July 16, 1861, McDowell's volunteer Union army marched south into Virginia. Many of the New Englanders, unaccustomed to the heat and humidity, grew faint and breathless, especially under the weight of their gear. They didn't keep in rank, and no number of orders could make them move faster. It took them two and a half days to go twenty-five miles.

Meanwhile, Confederate General Pierre Gustave Beauregard had been warned by Rose O'Neal Greenhow, a Southern spy living in Washington, D.C., that the Northern army was headed toward Richmond. Beauregard ordered his men to set up a line of resistance on one side of a creek called Bull Run, located not far from the railroad center at Manassas Junction.

Congressmen, senators, women, and children took positions on a hillside to watch the Union army — 37,000 strong — put an end to the rebellion. Almost a picnic atmosphere prevailed.

Spectators brought binoculars and lunch and sat on blankets under colorful parasols.

On Sunday, July 21, 1861, the two armies fought most of the day. At first it seemed to be going as General McDowell had planned, but holding a hill at the center of the Confederate line was a Virginian who was about to emerge a hero.

General Thomas J. Jackson believed that the Confederate cause was sacred and that his troops' chore was no less honorable than the Crusades. By the strength of his own conviction, Jackson was able to convince his men, who were generally from the hills and poor country, who owned no slaves, who grew no cotton, and who weren't well educated, that they had to save their homes and land from "Northern extremists." At Bull Run–Manassas, Jackson's line held like a stone wall. From that time until his death he was known as "Stonewall Jackson," one of the most brilliant field commanders in the war.

Union soldiers were not unified around one common cause. Their reasons for fighting were as diverse as the states they represented. A young man from Michigan might have taken up arms to preserve the Union. Another young man from Vermont might have worn the blue because he felt passionately about the abolition of slavery, while still another Union soldier, a Democrat and slaveholder from Maryland, had enlisted because it was his duty.

With so many degrees of commitment within the Union ranks, it is no wonder that when the battle turned and the South took the offensive, McDowell's men fled in confusion and chaos.

Seeing the Union army disintegrate in front of their eyes, watching in horror as they ran away, caused the spectators to panic. What seemed a certain victory turned into a demoralizing defeat. Jefferson Davis, who also had come to observe the battle, was delighted with the outcome. He and his staff declared a sure victory and the independence of a new nation. They had given the Union army a good whipping and now they could go home. They'd even captured a Yankee congressman, Albert Ely of New York, and taken him to Richmond as a prisoner of war.

When Lincoln received word that Union troops had broken ranks and that McDowell's army had been routed, he knew that

The Battle of Bull Run.
(Library of Congress)

saving the Union was not going to be achieved without the great loss of lives. The president was angry. He was sad. Some accounts say he wept.

Sergeant Elisha Hunt Rhodes from Rhode Island was in the battle that day. Rhodes wrote in his Civil War diary that although he had survived the first battle of Bull Run — known as "the Great Skedaddle" — he never thought he would. Admitting his personal terror, he said that during the fray he'd managed to hold on to his gun and cartridge box. "Many times," he remembered, "I sat down in the mud determined to go no further [sic], and willing to die to end my misery. But soon a friend would pass and urge me to make another effort, and I would stagger a mile further [sic]. At daylight we could see the spires of Washington." He would arrive in Washington in time to eat a cold breakfast in defeat.

"I well recollect when my master went to war. He called us all in the kitchen and told us he had to go over there and whip those [Yankees] and would be back 'fore breakfast. He didn't return for two years. I says, 'Master, we sure would have waited breakfast on you a long time.' He said, 'Yes, they's . . . hard to whip.'"

Slave Narrative

THE GENERAL
SAYS WE FREE

━━━◄◉►━━━

"If every son of a black mother had thrown 'way his hoe and took up a gun to fight for his own freedom along with the Yankees, the war'd been over before it began."
Slave Narrative

1862

Union soldiers freed Mary Barbour's family. Here's how she said it happened.

One night Mary's father gently shakes her shoulder. "Come on, Mary. Wake up, honey, we fixin' to go." The girl sleepily sits up, stretches, and yawns. It is the middle of the night. Where is Mama and Papa takin' us? she wonders.

"Light a candle," the girl whines, impatiently.

"No light," Papa answers, his voice strained by fear. "Dress in the dark."

Mama doesn't speak a word; she's busy putting a few necessary things in a sack. Mary's eyes are heavy. All she wants to do is fall back on her mat and sleep until the sun is high in the sky. But Papa's voice sounds anxious.

"Come on, chullun, we got to go now or never."

Mary's eyes finally adjust to the darkness in the cabin. She can see Mama waking the twins, who are still babies. Mama places a finger to her lips for them not to cry. The twins, who are just as confused as their older sister, obey without question.

Papa steps outside. He listens to the silence, and then he waves for the others to follow. Sneaking out of the house, being careful not to crack a twig, the fleeing family moves along the path. Papa is carrying one of the twins and holding Mary's hand. Mama has the other twin in her arms and the bundle slung over her shoulder. In a little while Papa leads them to the plum thicket where a mule and wagon are tied up.

The family climbs into the wagon. Mary is too scared to sleep now, but the twins cuddle on each side of Mama and go back to sleep. Nobody says a word as they travel all night.

Come morning light, the family reaches Union lines in New Bern. The Yankees confiscate the mule and wagon. "You're free now," say the soldiers in blue.

When Papa hears that, he offers his service as a shoemaker. "Through the war, my papa made Yankee boots, and we gits 'long pretty good," Mary Barbour ends her story, as told to an interviewer.

♦ ♦ ♦

The first battle went well for the rebels, but the Yankees weren't about to give up. The two armies dug in for a long, bitter winter.

Each side adopted its own songs that voiced its sentiments. "Dixie" was the anthem of the South, and the North embraced "The Battle Hymn of the Republic." A former slave remembered: "My old master . . . used to come to the Quarters and make us children sing. He make us sing 'Dixie.' Sometimes he make us sing half a day. Seems like 'Dixie' his main song. I tell you, I don't like it now. But have mercy, he made us sing it . . . I was glad when he went away to war and we didn't have to sing it no more."

> O, I wish I was in the land of cotton
> Old times there are not forgotten
> Look away! Look away! Look away! Dixie Land.
> In Dixie Land where I was born
> Early on one frosty mornin'
> Look away! Look away! Look away! Dixie Land.
> CHORUS:
> O, I wish I was in Dixie! Hooray! Hooray!
> In Dixie Land I'll take my stand
> To live and die in Dixie,
> Away, away, away down south in Dixie!
> Away, away, away down south in Dixie!

Julia Ward Howe, who helped her husband edit the antislavery journal *Boston Commonwealth,* wrote the words to "The Battle Hymn of the Republic." She was also an early feminist and supporter of universal suffrage.

Mine eyes have seen the glory of the
    coming of the Lord:
He is trampling out the vintage where the
    grapes of wrath are stored;
He hath loosed the fateful lightning of
    His terrible swift sword:
His truth is marching on.
CHORUS:
Glory! Glory! Hallelujah!
Glory! Glory! Hallelujah!
Glory! Glory! Hallelujah!
His truth is marching on.

Julia Ward Howe, poet, abolitionist, and social reformer. (Brown Brothers)

As the war progressed and the Union army began gaining territory in Southern states, slaves in these areas saw the military as an emancipating army and they bolted toward the sound of the shells and the drums. Since there wasn't a clear policy about what to do with runaways, it was often left up to the commanding officer to decide.

Union General George B. McClellan maintained the official government position, and announced that he would crush "any and all slave revolts." In fact, he wouldn't allow antislavery songs to be sung by entertainers who performed for his troops. And Major General John Dix, on seizing two counties in Virginia, was careful to order that slavery was not to be interfered with or slaves to be received into the line.

As fugitives reached federal lines, they offered their services as soldiers, laborers, and cooks. But they were often shocked and dismayed when some Union officers accepted them, but other officers ordered them turned away or captured and returned to their masters. Slaves were confused and angered when their rebel enemies were allowed to come behind Union lines to recapture "their property."

At Fortress Monroe, Virginia, abolitionist Major General Benjamin Butler got around the issue by declaring slaves "contraband" (confiscated property of the enemy) of war. He accepted runaways and put them to work. Butler reasoned that the Confederates used slaves to dig, cook, carry equipment, and clean, thereby helping the Confederate cause. Butler felt the Union could do the same thing, and eventually free those who cooperated. It was difficult to argue with his rationale.

At best it was a confusing situation, because there were plenty of officers and soldiers who refused to help runaways, but there were just as many antislavery commanders who helped.

Meanwhile, working in concert with the War Department,

Congress passed the first Confiscation Act in July 1861, freeing slaves who were being used by the Confederate military, but it didn't free slaves who might escape from slaveholders, or those in any of the loyal, slaveholding states — Missouri, Kentucky, Delaware, or Maryland. With this policy in place, slaves captured with Confederate soldiers could be freed and allowed to work for the Union. In this way some enslaved men and women celebrated their day of Jubilee before the Emancipation Proclamation: "Pre'dent Lincoln didn't free me. The General . . . tol' me I was free. Then he put me to work," reported a fugitive.

Loopholes in the first Confiscation Act allowed field officers to interpret it in different ways.

In Missouri there were pro-Confederate slaveholders who were openly defiant of federal authority. Major General John Charles Frémont of the Union's Western Department, headquartered in St. Louis, used the Confiscation Act to declare martial law and free the slaves of all disloyal slaveholders in Missouri, effective August 30, 1861.

President Lincoln was furious when he heard the news, but he tactfully asked Frémont to modify his order. Frémont refused and sent his wife, Jessie Frémont, the daughter of Senator Thomas Hart Benton of Missouri, to Washington to speak with the president about the matter.

President Lincoln greeted Jessie Frémont cordially, but he firmly let her know he was not going to let her husband's emancipation order stand. She went back to Missouri with the message. On

Major General John Charles Frémont. (Sophia Smith Collection, Smith College)

September 11, Lincoln told Frémont to lift his order or step down. Reluctantly, Frémont complied.

None of this internal struggle mattered to the slaves of Missouri. Once they heard about Frémont's order, they claimed their freedom behind Union lines and celebrated their day of Jubilee — albeit a brief one. To a handful of Missouri slaves the name of their emancipator was General John C. Frémont.

Frémont wasn't the only general who tried to free slaves within his jurisdiction. Major General David Hunter established the 1st Colored South Carolina Regiment. Then, using the authority stated in the Confiscation Act, he recruited runaways and began training them as soldiers. The War Department vehemently refused to support the venture, so it failed.

Then, on May 9, 1862, Major General Hunter freed all slaves in South Carolina, Georgia, and Florida.

Ten days later, Lincoln issued a proclamation nullifying the general's edict.

"I, Abraham Lincoln, President of the United States, proclaim and declare that . . . neither General Hunter, nor any other commander, or person, has been authorized by the Government of the United States to make proclamations declaring the slaves of any State free; and that the supposed proclamation now in question, whether genuine or false, is altogether void, so far as respects to declaration."

Lincoln also included a proposed gradual emancipation program with compensation to all slaveholders in loyal states. New Jersey and New York had used gradual emancipation to end slavery. President Lincoln believed that it was a good course of action at the time, and he followed up with a request that Congress appropriate funds to aid any state that accepted this offer.

Slaveholders in the loyal states were cool toward the proposal. And abolitionists bombarded the president's plan and criticized him for pandering to slaveholders. But President Lincoln was accustomed to being attacked because of his policies, which led him to say, "You can't fool all of the people all of the time."

HOPE IN
THE HEART

—◄●►—

"In the summer of 1862, freedmen began to flock into Washington from Maryland and Virginia. They came with [the] great hope in their hearts and with all their worldly goods on their backs. Fresh from the bonds of slavery, fresh from the benighted regions of the plantation, they came to the Capital looking for liberty, and many of them not knowing it when they found it . . ."

Elizabeth Keckley
Seamstress to Mrs. Lincoln

MARCH 1861

"Who are some of your other clients?" Mrs. Lincoln asks Elizabeth Keckley, during an interview at the White House. Since her arrival in Washington, Mary Lincoln has been searching for a seamstress. Mrs. McClean, a customer of Elizabeth's, has recommended her to the First Lady, who needs a dress for an affair the Tuesday after the inaugural.

"I've made dresses for Mrs. Jefferson Davis, Mrs. McClean, and a few other fine ladies of Washington," Mrs. Keckley answers. "I haven't been in Washington very long, having come from St. Louis where I had a larger clientele. Before that I was a slave."

"I know of your work," says Mrs. Lincoln. "But I will not pay high prices just because I am the First Lady. If you are fair with me, you will have all the work you can possibly handle."

The two women negotiate and come to terms that are fair to both parties. Mrs. Lincoln commissions a dress made of a rose-colored antique moiré, but it has to be finished by the end of the following week. An almost impossible job.

Happy to get the assignment, Mrs. Keckley accepts the terms. She works night and day and even hires a lady to help in the cutting and pressing of the garment. Elizabeth is determined to get the job done . . . and done well. She knows that her career as a seamstress is depending on the outcome of this very special dress.

Tuesday evening comes, the night of the big affair. Mrs. Keckley has just finished putting the last stitches on the hem. A carriage is waiting outside to rush her to the White House. Swishing hurriedly inside the White House with the folded dress over her arms, she is escorted upstairs where Mrs. Lincoln is impatient and angry. She is furious with "Lizzie."

Mrs. Keckley wonders what the matter is. What has she done?

"You have failed me," Mrs. Lincoln wails. "You are a total disappointment and I am bitterly angry. You are late and I cannot possibly get dressed."

> *But there is plenty of time.* Why is the First Lady behaving like a spoiled child, *Elizabeth wonders? Then she decides that perhaps Mrs. Lincoln is suffering from a case of nerves, and not really angry about anything she has done.* "Oh, Mrs. Lincoln," *Elizabeth says quietly.* "Trust me. You have plenty of time. I personally will dress you and everything will be just fine."
>
> *The First Lady calms down as Elizabeth arranges her hair and helps her into the lovely dress she has made. It fits nicely.*
>
> *Suddenly the door swings open and the president steps in. He casually throws himself on the sofa.* "I declare, Mother, you look charming in that dress."
>
> *That's all it takes. The smile on Mrs. Lincoln's face lights up the room. And Mrs. Keckley knows that she will sew for Mrs. Lincoln again.*

Slaves living in Washington, D.C., celebrated their day of Jubilee on April 16, 1862, when Congress voted to abolish slavery and pay loyal slave owners compensation for loss of their property. There was even more cause to be happy when Congress prohibited slavery in the territories on June 19, 1862.

Abolitionists scoffed at the idea of paying slaveholders to free their slaves, because it placed human beings in the same category as livestock and household goods. But to those slaves involved, freedom was freedom and they embraced it without question. Their initial response was to celebrate joyously.

Bands played. Children sang. Church bells rang. Black churches were filled, and black speakers thanked God for allowing them to live to see the great day of deliverance.

When the excitement of Jubilee wore off, though, the freedmen were left with the reality of their situation. They were in Washington homeless and penniless. They were living in squalor, eating what they could beg or steal, wearing rags, and using any materials they could to construct makeshift housing. A year after slavery had ended in Washington, D.C., there were an estimated 10,000 black refugees crowded into the city and in Alexandria, Virginia, which was under Union military control. (By the war's end there would be 40,000 former slaves living within the District of Columbia and surrounding areas.)

Who could help them? Who would?

Elizabeth Keckley, a former slave herself, was now Mrs. Lincoln's dressmaker and traveling companion. Mrs. Keckley wanted to do something to help the freedmen, and she felt it was partly the responsibility of free African Americans

Elizabeth Keckley, seamstress to Mrs. Lincoln. (Moorland–Spingam Research Center, Howard University, Washington, D.C.)

to shepherd their brothers and sisters until they were able to fend for themselves.

"The thought was ever present with me," Mrs. Keckley wrote in her autobiography, "and the next Sunday I made a suggestion in the colored church, that a society of colored people be formed to labor for the benefit of the freedmen. The idea proved popular, and in two weeks the Contraband Relief Association was organized with forty willing members."

While visiting New York with the First Lady, Mrs. Keckley told her about the project. Mrs. Lincoln approved of it and donated two hundred dollars. While traveling to Boston with Mrs. Lincoln, Mrs. Keckley used the opportunity to meet the well-known abolitionists Wendell Phillips and Frederick Douglass, each of whom also donated two hundred dollars. President Lincoln made a personal contribution for the benefit of the relief society, and Mrs. Lincoln donated more money and encouraged cabinet wives to do the same.

The first lady, Mary Todd Lincoln. (Meserve–Kunhardt Collection)

Another supporter of the Washington, D.C., refugees was Harriet Jacobs, who had claimed her own personal Jubilee by running away. She joined Mrs. Keckley in her efforts to assist those who had made their way to freedom and needed help.

Clearly the private sector could not carry the full responsibility of caring for the ex-slaves. They needed a federally funded program. After extensive lobbying by abolitionists, the War Department established the American Freedmen's Inquiry Commission in 1863. Its purpose was to investigate the needs of ex-slaves and recommend plans for their transition from bondage to freedom as smoothly as possible. Based on those findings, the Freedmen's Bureau finally was established in 1865.

President Lincoln's first year in office was spent trying to stay focused on saving the Union. His generals were ineffective and he was often in conflict with his cabinet and congressional leaders regarding policy. Abolitionists were opposed to his gradual emancipation-with-compensation plan and loyal slaveholders were constantly using the threat of secession to get their way. Lincoln endured it all with a quiet grace, until his son Willie died of "a fever" during the winter of 1862. The president and his wife were devastated by the death of their son. By all accounts, the Lincolns became overprotective of their son Tad, and by the president's own admission he spoiled the child because, "I just can't say no to the boy."

Each time reports of war casualties

President Lincoln with his son Tad.
(Library of Congress)

came in, Lincoln suffered as though Willie had just died a thousand times over. The president's tall, gaunt figure could be seen pensively pacing the halls of the White House, wearing his grief like an ill-fitting shroud, soaked in the blood of patriots too numerous to count. This terrible sorrow enveloped Lincoln's whole being until his own death finally released him from it.

Privately, the first months of 1862 were sad and anxious days for the Lincoln family. Mrs. Keckley wrote:

"One day [the president] came into the room where I was fitting a dress on Mrs. Lincoln. His step was slow and heavy, and his face sad. Like a tired child he threw himself upon a sofa, and shaded his eyes with his hands. He was a complete picture of dejection. He sat and read the Bible for a while, after which he seemed to be relieved . . . He was reading the Book of Job."

Yet even in his grief, the president calmly went about the business of governing the war-torn country. He had selected George B. McClellan in the summer of 1861 to lead the Union army in the East. McClellan, a Democrat, was a thirty-five-year-old veteran of the Mexican War and not very respectful of the president. When warned of McClellan's political ambition and arrogance, Lincoln responded, "Never mind, I will hold [his] stirrups if he will bring us victory." Lincoln often used his wit to camouflage his frustration, especially when it involved his generals.

Meanwhile, the debate over slavery was persistent and gaining momentum. In July 1862, Congress passed the Militia Act, which provided for the employment of "persons of African descent to be used by the military for any service for which they might be found competent." The act also granted freedom to "slaves so employed and to their families if their owners belonged to a disloyal family."

President Lincoln modified his emancipation plan, targeting the year 1900 the official end of slavery. Each slaveholder would receive three hundred to four hundred dollars from the government for each slave he freed. Then these freed slaves were to be sent, at the government's expense, to locales in Africa, South America, or the Caribbean.

According to minutes of a meeting between the president and a group of prominent black businessmen and community leaders, including Frederick Douglass, Lincoln said, "Our white men are cutting one another's throats . . . but for your race among us there could not be war . . . It is better for us both, therefore, to be separated." The president then shared his colonization policy with them.

Later, Isaiah Wears, a free black Philadelphian, responded angrily, "To be asked after so many years of oppression and wrong . . . to pull up stakes . . . and go . . . is unreasonable." Later, Frederick Douglass denounced the policy in a scathing editorial.

◆ ◆ ◆

". . . [B]y this time every man who has an ounce of brain in his head, no matter to which party he may belong, and even Mr. Lincoln himself, must know quite well that the mere presence of the colored race never could have provoked this horrid and desolating rebellion. No, Mr. President, it is not the innocent horse that makes the horse thief, not the traveler's purse that makes a highway robber, and it is not the presence of the Negro that causes this foul and unnatural war, but the cruel and brutal cupidity of those who wish to possess horses, money, and Negroes by means of theft, robbery, and rebellion."

THE NORTH STAR

I HAVE MADE UP MY MIND

＝＞((()))⇐＝

"When you are dead and in Heaven, in a thousand years that action of yours will make the Angels sing your praises."

HANNAH JOHNSON
Daughter of a fugitive slave
In a letter to President Lincoln

SPRING 1862

    Charles Sumner limps down the steps, leaning on the arm of his friend Congressman Thaddeus Stevens from Philadelphia, Pennsylvania. Both are helped into the awaiting carriage that will drive them the short distance to the War Department. They have been scheduled to meet with the president before noon. Once again they will try to persuade Lincoln to do what they believe to be morally right and politically sound — abolish slavery.

    Senator Charles Sumner, Republican from Massachusetts, has been against slavery longer than most of his colleagues have lived. A Harvard-educated scholar, he is unequaled in the Senate for his passionate oration against slavery. And he has paid the price for it.

On May 19, 1856, Sumner had given a strong speech against pro-slavery elements in the Senate. Three days later while the senator was sitting at his desk, Preston Brooks, a South Carolina representative, entered the senate chamber and attacked Sumner with a cane. Although it took him three years to recover from the assault and even now he still limps, he refuses to retreat one step from his position that slavery is "evil and has to be abolished."

Thaddeus Stevens is called the "Great Commoner" because he feels that poor whites also suffer from prejudices and injustices. But they have been made to believe that they are somehow better off because they are neither black nor slaves. Stevens argues that, without an economic base, poor people — white and black — are powerless, and neither of them can ever be really free. Sumner and Stevens are so hated that a wealthy Mississippian has placed a bounty of one hundred dollars on their heads — dead or alive.

Among those who pushed Lincoln the hardest regarding emancipation were Massachusetts Senator Charles Sumner and Congressman Thaddeus Stevens from Philadelphia. "You must act now," said Stevens repeatedly.

Fear of foreign intervention in the war influenced President

Lincoln to take action. The Confederacy had assumed, mistakenly, that the demand for cotton from textile mills would lead Britain to help the Confederacy by breaking the Union naval blockade. Redefining the war as one against slavery might generate support from England and France. Both countries had ended slavery, and they each had very powerful abolitionist organizations calling for the end of American slavery. By the summer of 1862, Lincoln also realized that freeing some slaves to save the Union might be a necessary war measure for suppressing the rebellion. It was also within his constitutional authority as the commander in chief of the military to take the action he was planning.

Senator Charles Sumner, Republican from Massachusetts. (Library of Congress)

On July 18, 1862, the president rode to the Soldiers' Home with Vice President Hannibal Hamlin. After the ride and a meal, Lincoln shared a rough draft of an emancipation proclamation with him. Lincoln braced for criticism from Hamlin, who was from Vermont and had abolitionist leanings. Instead, the vice president said, "There is no criticism to be made."

Based on the diaries of several cabinet members, the idea of emancipation wasn't received enthusiastically. The war wasn't going well for the North at the time. Morale was poor, and midterm elections were coming up. Lincoln's ratings were very low and steadily dropping with each military defeat. So, it was suggested that before issuing any such proclamation there needed to be a big Northern victory.

President Lincoln was a shrewd politician who had the ability to read the mood of the people around him. He tabled the idea, but left his cabinet with the compelling argument that General Hunter had presented to him some months earlier: "Freeing the slaves in the rebel states is a military necessity, absolutely essential to the preservation of the Union. The slaves are a source of strength to the South, and we must decide whether that element should be with us or against us."

President Lincoln kept the proclamation in his desk drawer all summer, until finally McClellan gave the North a much-needed victory on September 17 at Antietam (Sharpsburg), Maryland. Won at the high cost of 5,000 dead and 20,000 wounded, it was enough for Lincoln to move ahead with his emancipation plan.

On September 22, 1862, the president read the Emancipation Proclamation to his cabinet, to become effective January 1, 1863. He said, according to Secretary Chase's diary:

"I determined, as soon as [the Rebel army] should be driven out of Maryland, to issue a Proclamation of Emancipation such as I thought most likely to be useful. I said nothing to anyone; but I made the promise to myself, and . . . my Maker. The Rebel army is now driven out, and I am going to fulfill that promise. I have got you together to hear what I have written down. I do not wish your advice about the main matter — for that I have determined for myself."

When the Emancipation Proclamation was made public in

September, the response was mixed. It wasn't the document many had hoped for, but it was praised for being a brilliant military move on the part of Lincoln. Many abolitionists were critical of it, saying it was useless and essentially freed no one. Others such as Thaddeus Stevens and Charles Sumner cheered the proclamation as a promise of things to come. Stevens felt the executive order issued by the president paved the way for Congress to introduce an amendment to the Constitution ending slavery. A few years earlier, such a suggestion would have been met with opposition from as many Northerners as Southerners. But passage of an emancipation amendment didn't seem so farfetched anymore. Getting it ratified might take more effort.

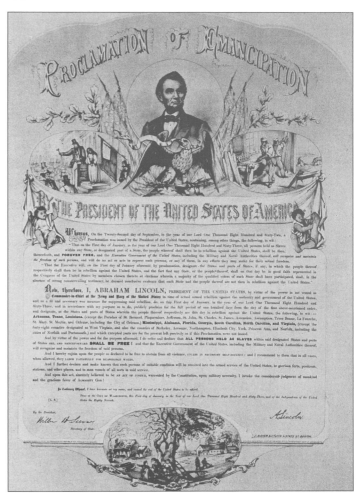

The Emancipation Proclamation. (National Archives and Records Administration)

The proposed emancipation by the president was met with vicious opposition from Southerners, as was expected. Slaveholders weren't going to obey Lincoln's proclamation, but they feared that their slaves, upon hearing that they had been freed, might rise up in rebellion.

John Hay, the president's secretary, wrote in his diary after observing the president and his cabinet members at a reception following the release of the first draft: "They all seemed to feel a sort of new and exhilarated life; they breathed freer; the President's Proclamation had freed them as well as the slaves."

Frederick Douglass found hope in the fact that Lincoln added a clause that opened the army to African Americans. At last blacks would get to fight for their own freedom, a cause for which Douglass had lobbied.

A lot could happen between September and January, so the abolitionists remained on guard until the New Year.

STOMP
IT DOWN

=►((◊))◄=

"There are certain great national acts which, by their relation to universal principles, properly belong to the whole human family, and Abraham Lincoln's proclamation of the first of January, 1863, is one of these acts. Henceforth that day shall take rank with the Fourth of July. Henceforth it becomes the date of a new and glorious era in the history of American liberty. Henceforth it shall stand associated in the minds of men with all those stately steps of mankind . . ."

FREDERICK DOUGLASS
January 1, 1863

DECEMBER 31, 1862

Watch Night

There is some fear — especially among the abolitionists — that Lincoln might be persuaded not to sign the emancipation. So, on New Year's Eve, all over the world, people are watching and waiting prayerfully. Will he sign the long-awaited emancipation order? Surely he will. Surely he must.

In London, England, several thousand working-class men are meeting to denounce slavery and to support the emancipation of American slaves. In Canada, runaways are gathered to count the hours until they finally will be free and can return to their homeland and reunite their families.

As the evening progresses, groups of people continue meeting, even though there is a raging winter storm under way in the Northeast. A former slave who is now a preacher in a Boston church speaks to a racially mixed congregation, saying, ". . . We all know that evil is 'round the President. While we sit here, they are trying to make him break his word. But we have come to this Watch Night to see that he does not break his word." The preacher, a tall, inky-black man with a voice that can shake the very foundations of Hades, tells his audience that the "ol' Serpent" will use all of his power to stop the signing of the Emancipation Proclamation. To those in that room, slaveholders and those who support the evil system are considered the agents of Satan, whose name is often "the Serpent."

"But don't be scared," the preacher says. "We'll pray . . . and God Almighty's New Year will make the United States the land of the free!"

People cry and moan in the flickering candlelight. They sink to their knees and hum, clap their hands, or hold their bodies still from violent, emotional shaking.

A minute or two before midnight, a group of people begin making a hissing sound symbolically representing that Satan is *near. The sound grows louder by degree. As the bloodcurdling hissing fills the room, the preacher yells, "He is here!" The preacher's voice can be heard above the chilling hisses, admonishing evil and calling for deliverance and freedom.*

With a wave of his hand, the preacher casts the Evil One and all his emissaries into the Pit of Fire and proclaims freedom for all men and women regardless of color.

People are shouting, crying, begging God's mercy for those held in bondage.

Suddenly the first toll of the twelfth hour begins. At the twelfth strike, the hissing stops. The preacher's words stop. But his face is glowing with triumph. There is not a person who leaves this place who does not believe that President Lincoln will sign the Emancipation Proclamation on this day, the first day of January 1863.

On New Year's morning after a fitful night's sleep, Lincoln sat at his White House desk and put the finishing touches on the document that would earn him the title of "Emancipator." Lincoln's hands were trembling so; he could hardly hold the pen. Perhaps it was because he had been shaking hands all morning and his muscles were fatigued. Perhaps it was the weight of what he was doing that made him tremble. And there are even a few who believe —

though Lincoln denied it — that he shook because he wasn't sure about his decision and "trembled in response to the conflict that was raging inside him." For whatever reason, the president steadied his hand and signed himself into history. *Abraham Lincoln.* In fact, he said, "If my name ever goes into history, it will be for this act."

In reality the Emancipation Proclamation could not be enforced. And it left 830,000 people enslaved in the border states. Even so, on January 1, 1863, blacks and abolitionists celebrated everywhere. Their rejoicing was uncomplicated and straightforward. "We was slaves one day. We was free the next," said Tyus Greer, who was freed by the proclamation in Union-held territory.

Long before President Lincoln dipped his pen in the inkwell, celebrations had already begun. On the evening of January 1, a grand Jubilee concert was held at Boston's Music Hall where the leading abolitionist and literary figures of the day sang, made speeches, and rejoiced to the sounds of Carl Zerrahn's Philharmonic Orchestra playing Beethoven's Fifth Symphony. To climax the evening, a chorus sang Mendelssohn's "Hymn of Praise."

Seven bells tolled the hour. The winter storm that pummeled the city with several inches of new snow had passed. The weather had not dampened the enthusiasm of the crowd that had gathered at Boston's Tremont Baptist Church. The packed snow crunched under the feet of people rushing toward the church. Their faces were aglow. Their eyes were happy. Only something wonderful could make people look this way. Entering the church, a woman took ten cents from her purse and paid for her entry. It was a reasonable fee for the cost of the program. Besides, Frederick Douglass was supposed to speak that night.

After hours of long-winded speeches, a messenger burst through the door. "It is coming! It is on the wires!" A thunderous cheer exploded and spilled out into the street. The president had signed the Emancipation Proclamation. Jubilee! Jubilee! Everybody joined in as Douglass's rich baritone voice roared, "Blow ye the trumpet, blow." Jubilee! Jubilee!

Besides the meeting at Tremont Baptist Church, there were other gatherings among free blacks in Philadelphia, Cincinnati, New York, and Washington, D.C.

In Washington, close to 600 black men, women, and children who lived in the temporary barracks known as "Contraband Camp" held a "night watch" the evening before the signing of the proclamation. Superintendent D. B. Nichols reported that they prayed, sang, and told stories about their days in slavery. The newly freed blacks seemed quiet, reflective, and reverent. "No mo' dat!" said a former slave named Thornton. "No mo' dat! No mo' slavery!"

A few minutes before midnight, all the people dropped to their knees and prayed silently. Then, as the hour struck twelve, their mood and attitude changed. They commenced to singing and dancing and shouting that there would be "no mo' dat!"

In Union-held Southern territory, contraband slaves got the message that they were free on January 1. Traditionally the first day of the year had been "selling-off day" on the plantation. Fathers

Emancipation Day celebration in Washington, D.C., January 1, 1863. (Granger Collection, New York)

and mothers were hired out or sold away from their children or vice versa. In the Sea Islands off the coast of South Carolina, ex-slaves celebrated their freedom during the winter of '63 in the simple knowledge that they couldn't be separated from one another again. They hugged their children and wept tears of relief.

One South Carolina slave, freed by the proclamation, recalled that on the first Sunday of Freedom, "Sister Carrie, who was near 'bout a hundred, started in to talkin':

> *'Tain't no mo' sellin' today.*
> *Tain't no mo' hirin' today.*
> *Tain't no mo' pullin' off shirts today.*
> *It's stomp down Freedom today.*
> *Stomp it down.'"*

Then the whole congregation stood up, formed a circle, and began to stomp and clap as they repeated the phrase over and over.

"Stomp down Freedom today.

Stomp it down!

Stomp down Freedom today.

Stomp it down!"

In the loyal states, slavery was still a legal institution, protected by the Constitution. A few masters in Missouri, Maryland, Kentucky, and Delaware freed their slaves in the "spirit" of the proclamation, but those instances were rare.

It didn't matter whether the slaves lived in a rebel state or a loyal state, once they got word that *some* of them were free, they counted themselves in that number and left from wherever they were and headed toward Union lines. They fled in droves. Many of them escaped via the Underground Railroad, which was still making regular runs — especially in the border states and even throughout the Deep South. In Missouri, for example, there were 114,931 slaves reported in the 1860 census. Only 73,811 remained in 1863; the decrease was credited to escapes. Newspapers from that time were filled with notices of

Slaves being liberated by black troops.

rewards for the return of runaways. The Canton, Missouri, *Press* reported in the July 16, 1863, edition that a group of three men, three women, and six children had escaped, crossing into Iowa, which was called "Negro Paradise."

Unfortunately, millions of slaves living under the Confederate flag spent January 1, 1863, with no knowledge of their freedom. Slavery was a crumbling institution whose days were numbered. But not soon enough for the ones who were still left waiting for their day of Jubilee.

Slaveholders never mentioned the Emancipation Proclamation until they had to. But when the slaves found out, they moved out . . .

"We done heared dat [Lincoln] gonna turn de slaves free. Ole missus say there warn't nothing to it. Then a Yankee soldier tol' someone in Williamsburg that Marse Lincoln done signed de 'mancipation. Was wintertime an' mighty cold dat night, but ev'ybody commence gettin' ready to leave. Didn't care nothin' 'bout Missus — was goin' to Union lines. An' all dat night the slaves danced and sang right out in the cold. Nex' morning at day-break we all started out with blankets an' clothes an' pots and pans an' chickens piled on our backs, 'cause Missus said we couldn't take no horses or carts."

Slave Narrative

I'M FREE AND I'M COMIN' TO FREE YOU

"Union forever
Hurrah, boys, hurrah!
Although I may be po'
I aine a slave no mo'
Shouting the battle cry of freedom."
                    Soldier's marching song
                    Slave Narrative

Slaves serve as crew members aboard private ships used for Confederate purposes. Robert Smalls is a pilot on the Planter, a cotton steamer converted into a rebel vessel.

At half past three o'clock in the morning on May 13, 1862, Smalls leaves the Atlantic Dock with the Planter. He sails to where the Ettaone is docked. Guided only by moonlight, he quietly slips his family and several other families on board. Next, Smalls proceeds down Charleston River very slowly. When opposite Fort Johnson, he gives two long blasts on his horn, the signal that he is expected to give. All is well. Smalls goes undetected and he is able to pass unhindered.

> *On reaching Fort Sumter at 4 A.M., he gives another signal, which is answered from the fort, thereby giving Smalls permission to pass. No one yet realizes that Smalls is in command of the vessel. As soon as he clears the last vessel that might have stopped him, Smalls speeds for the Union blockading fleet. By the time anyone realizes what is happening, the* Planter *is entirely out of range of Sumter's guns.*
>
> *Smalls hoists a white flag, and at 5 A.M. reaches a Union blockade vessel where he turns over his prize. Admiral Dupont calls Smalls's victory "one of the coolest and most gallant Naval acts of war."*

The Emancipation Proclamation transformed the Union army into a liberating force, and black soldiers were going to be allowed to fight for that cause. One of the first things ex-slaves did with their freedom was to join the army. They were not fighting to save the Union only, but to bring Jubilee to all their people. And on this issue they were firmly committed and determined to see it through to the end or die trying.

Altogether about 186,000 black soldiers served in the Union army and another 29,000 in the navy. This accounted for about 10 percent of all Union forces. Of the black soldiers more than 68,178 were dead or missing at the end of the war. Twenty-four African

Americans received the Congressional Medal of Honor for bravery in battle.

But in the beginning, black soldiers were not respected or treated fairly by white officers. Some white officers such as Robert Gould Shaw, commander of the legendary 54th Massachusetts Regiment, were proud to lead black troops in battle. Others were not. Then on May 13, 1862, Robert Smalls, a slave, shattered the notion that black men would not act nobly in a battlefront situation, when he seized the *Planter* and sailed it to Union-held territory. Turning the vessel over to Union officer Admiral Samuel F. Dupont, the fugitive sailor said, "I thought the *Planter* might be of some use to Uncle Abe."

Union hero Robert Smalls.
(Library of Congress)

Aside from being criticized and having their ability and courage questioned, African American soldiers were punished more severely than their white counterparts for the slightest infraction. Faced with all kinds of opposition and discrimination, blacks were paid less for the same risk as well.

For example, a white private was paid thirteen dollars a month and three dollars and fifty cents for clothing. Blacks were paid ten dollars a month and received a three-dollar clothing allowance. Blacks who protested were subject to cruel and unusual punishment. Sergeant William Walker, of the 3rd South Carolina Volunteers, led a group of protesters who refused to perform duties until the black soldiers were paid equal wages. The entire company was charged with mutiny and Walker was executed. On January 1, 1864, Congress finally passed a law "equalizing pay, arms, equipment, and medical services for black troops," though it was not retroactive.

Confederates hated black soldiers, who were more likely to be killed than taken prisoners of war, or left to die if wounded. The Fort Pillow Massacre in Tennessee illustrated this extremism.

In the spring of 1864, Confederate forces under the command of General Nathan Bedford Forrest, often described by historians as a very capable officer but ruthless by nature, captured Fort Pillow, on the Mississippi River, where at least 300 blacks and their officers had surrendered. According to an official report by the army, Confederate soldiers under Forrest's command butchered the captives "like cattle — clubbing the wounded to death, burning some alive, and nailing others to the walls." In all the war, this was the most horrible of atrocities, except perhaps for the prison camp, Andersonville, in Georgia. Northern newspapers labeled Forrest "Butcher Forrest." Less than a week after the massacre, 1,200 black troops in Memphis took a solemn oath to avenge their brothers. "Remember Fort Pillow!" became their battle cry.

When black soldiers continued to fight bravely and when they began making a difference in the outcome of important battles, public opinion slowly shifted and the black soldier got the praise and respect he deserved. President Lincoln was the first to issue words of encouragement to the "colored troops," whom he at first believed were too timid to fight.

A Union captain expressed his admiration in the following report:

"A great many [white people] have the idea that the entire Negro race are vastly inferior. A few weeks of calm, unprejudiced life here would disadvise them, I think. I have a more elevated opinion of their abilities than I ever had before. I know how many of them are vastly the superiors of those . . . who would condemn them to a life of brutal degradation."

In the North and South, women also aided the war effort by raising money, collecting clothing, or gathering food. Dorothea Dix was selected by the War Department to be the superintendent of nurses in the Union army. Clara Barton took medicine and supplies to the battlefield and nursed wounded soldiers. Mary Ann Bickerdyke worked for better sanitation and nutrition in Union hospitals. African American women also served both the Union and Confederate armies as nurses, cooks, and spies.

Among the black women who worked for the Union cause was Harriet Tubman, the best-known conductor on the Underground Railroad. She remained an active conductor throughout the war years, and single-handedly brought hundreds of men out of slavery and into federal forces. As a master of disguise she served as a spy

Harriet Tubman and a few of the many slaves she helped to free. (Sophia Smith Collection, Smith College)

and encouraged other conductors to serve in that capacity as well.

Soldiers on the Sea Islands freed Susie King, born a slave in Georgia. She married Edward King, also a former slave, who was a sergeant in the U.S. 1st South Carolina Volunteers. As a nurse she earned the respect of both blacks and whites.

Sojourner Truth, a former slave in New York who had become a well-known feminist and abolitionist, often visited black soldiers camped near her Battle Creek, Michigan, home. In their honor she wrote verses that were sung to the tune of "The Battle Hymn of the Republic":

♦ ♦ ♦

We are done with hoeing cotton;

    we are done with hoeing corn;

We are colored Yankee soldiers;

    as sure as you are born.

When Massa hears us shouting,

    he will think 'tis Gabriel's horn

As we go marching on.

Charlotte Forten, a granddaughter of James Forten, also came south to support the war effort. She helped ex-slaves on the Georgia Sea Islands build houses and start schools and businesses, and instructed them in basic nutrition and hygiene. She said, "I never before saw children so eager to learn, although I had had several years' experience in New England schools. Coming to school is a constant delight and recreation to them. They come here as other children go to play."

Countless unnamed women of color volunteered as cooks and laundresses and nursed the sick, while scores of others cleaned weapons, sewed, or wove baskets.

Black women played an important role in helping the Confederacy. Southern black women, collectively called "Confederate Mary," gained the trust of Union soldiers, then smuggled medicine and delivered messages to the rebels.

Sojourner Truth.
(Bentley Historical Society,
University of Michigan)

These black women seemed not to be motivated by political or military reasons, but rather loyalty to or fear of their white masters and neighbors. James Gill, a former slave in Alabama, explained in a slave narrative that his mother assisted a group of Confederate soldiers separated from their unit behind enemy territory because ". . . they was us closest neighbors and some of them lived on join-ing places." Gill said his mother cooked for rebel soldiers and hid them. "None of the Yankees knowed that Mammy was a Confederate."

Black soldier.
(North Wind Picture Archive)

By the end of the war, at least 3,200 women had served both armies.

Slaves described black troops as a band of angels or saints because they brought the good news of free-dom. They welcomed them by dancing, shouting, and clapping. But sometimes white Yankees were mis-trusted, and with good reason. Not all Yankees came to the South with good feelings toward blacks. The slave narratives are filled with stories about Union troops who were mean and ornery. They took horses, mules, hogs, chickens — everything — then burned the only homes the slaves had ever known. Slaves learned from these actions that Northern whites were no different than Southern whites: Some were mean-spirited, unkind, ungrateful, and foolish, too.

"I suppose them Yankees was all right in their place," began one narrative, ". . . but they never belonged in the South. When one of them asked me what was them white flowers in the field, you'd think that a gentleman with all them decorations on hisself woulda knowed he was looking at a field of cotton."

The narratives are also rich with stories about white Yankees who were compassionate and sincere.

"I was nursin' my baby when I heared a gallopin', and 'fore I could move, here come de Yankees ridin' up . . . He lean't over an' patted de baby on he head an' ast what was his name. I tol' him it was Charlie, like his father. Then he ast, 'Charlie what?' an' I tol' him Charlie Sparks. Then he reach in his pocket an' pull out a copper an' say, 'Well you sure have a purty baby. Buy him something with this; an' thankee fo' the direction. Good-bye, Mrs. Sparks.' Now, what do you think of that? They all call me 'Mrs. Sparks'!"

NO TIME FOR
TEARS OUT HERE

———✦———

"Along evening, I's hear guns shooting. I sure am scared this time. Sure 'nough . . . [then] I hears two men say, 'Stick yo' hands up, boy. What you doing?' I says, 'Uh, uh-uh, I dunno. You aine gwine take me back to the plantation, is you?' They says, 'No. Does you want to fight for the North?' I says I will 'cause they talks like they northern men . . . They put me to work helping pull and set the cannons."

THOMAS COLE
Jackson County, Alabama
Slave Narrative

JULY 3, 1863

Gettysburg Battlefield

Elisha Hunt Rhodes has been fighting for two days. His bones are tired. His mind feels scrambled like a dozen eggs. But he must try to stay focused. Nobody in the 2nd Rhode Island Volunteers has been killed but five have been wounded. He can still hear their painful cries for help; they're pleading for death to come and relieve them of their awful suffering. The smell of blood-soaked mud makes Elisha's stomach churn, but he has been given an order to report to the line held by General Birney.

Moving from tree to tree, hiding behind stones and shrubs, he and his brigade make their way to the appointed destination. The constant booming of cannons makes his head hurt, but he has no time to worry about such a minor discomfort. There is a hailstorm of flying rock and pieces of metal falling all around him. He trips over a fallen comrade, but regains his balance and moves on. It is noon, but the sun is blocked by gunpowder mixed with dark overhanging clouds. Humidity hovers like a smothering rag and the stench is revolting.

Suddenly, Rhodes hears the rebel yell. The enemy is coming, running full force. He doesn't remember much more — just fighting, fighting to live one more day. For him to live someone else has to die. The idea is against his gentler nature, so he must allow his survival instincts to take over.

When the fighting is over, Rhodes removes his diary from his pack. His hand is still unsteady, but he writes about his experience here at Gettysburg. When he finishes, he collapses in a heap and falls asleep amid the dead and dying.

The Emancipation Proclamation shifted the war from being about preserving the Union to one that also included freedom. Some Northerners weren't willing to fight to free black people. Others were. Families divided along ideological lines when brothers chose to fight or not to fight for opposing sides.

The South was holding its own on the battlefield, while Lincoln was struggling with his generals. Union defeats at Fredericksburg and Chancellorsville gave General Robert E. Lee the momentum he needed to invade the North. Lee believed that a well-timed Confederate victory on Northern soil would bring about a speedy end to the war and also persuade England and France to acknowledge the legitimacy of the Confederate government.

General Robert E. Lee.
(Library of Congress)

As Lee's army moved through the Shenandoah Valley and headed for Harrisburg, Pennsylvania, Union General George Meade was charged with stopping the advance. On July 1, 1863, the two armies met near the farming town of Gettysburg.

The first three days of July 1863, Lee threw everything he had at the Union, but his attempts were unsuccessful. Then on the afternoon of July 3, Major General George Pickett led 15,000 soldiers against the Union defense — known as "Pickett's Charge." It ended in a crushing defeat for Pickett.

When the sun rose on the Fourth of July, the North claimed a victory. But at what cost? They had stopped Lee's advance, yet more than 50,000 soldiers lay dead — blacks and whites, death being the equalizer. Many of these young men had been unable to write their names or read a newspaper;

some had never been more than twenty miles from their homes; some had lived in large cities, others had lived on rural farms. All of them had believed in the cause for which they were fighting. On this day, all the rhetoric that had brought them to this place seemed futile. Where was the sense of it all? None of the young men — average age nineteen — who died at Gettysburg would ever anticipate Christmas or celebrate a birthday, get married or see sweet home again. The loss was incomprehensible. And none mourned for them more than President Lincoln.

The bodies were hastily buried to help control cholera and other diseases that were taking more lives than bullets. There wasn't even time to cry. "No time for tears out here," a young journalist wrote.

To keep the war effort going, the administration needed soldiers and money, so Congress passed a law to which Lincoln signed on March 3, 1863, authorizing the draft. Men who were the sole support of women and children were exempt. If a man was willing to pay a three-hundred-dollar fee to the government, or if he could find a substitute who would fight in his place, he could avoid the draft. Objection to the war was not grounds for exemption. Tensions over the law led to the worst mob violence in American history. It began in New York City on July 11, 1863, days after the Battle of Gettysburg.

Irish immigrants, angry about the draft and also fearful of losing their jobs to freed slaves, ruthlessly murdered at least a dozen African American men and destroyed draft offices. They burned and looted black neighborhoods and the homes of leading

> **Executive Mansion,**
>
> Washington,   , 186 .
>
> Four score and seven years ago our fathers brought forth, upon this continent, a new nation, conceived in liberty, and dedicated to the proposition that "all men are created equal"
>
> Now we are engaged in a great civil war, testing whether that nation, or any nation so conceived, and so dedicated, can long endure. We are met on a great battle field of that war. We have come to dedicate a portion of it, as a final resting place for those who died here, that the nation might live. This we may, in all propriety do. But, in a larger sense, we can not dedicate— we can not consecrate— we can not hallow, this ground— The brave men, living and dead, who struggled here, have hallowed it, far above our poor power to add or detract. The world will little note, nor long remember what we say here; while it can never forget what they did here.
>
> It is rather for us, the living, to stand here,

First draft of the Gettysburg Address. (New-York Historical Society)

Republicans and abolitionists. Eventually soldiers, straight from the battlefield at Gettysburg, were sent to restore order. Police and soldiers killed about 120 people.

At the dedication of the battlefield cemetery at Gettysburg, on November 19, 1863, more than 50,000 people listened to President Lincoln give a two-minute speech containing just ten sentences, yet it was unequaled in power, grace, and dignity. In the Gettysburg Address, President Lincoln left no doubt that he was now committed to preserving a free nation, "conceived in Liberty and dedicated to the proposition that all men are created equal."

Meanwhile, President Lincoln looked to the west for the military leadership he needed. While General Lee was being stopped at Gettysburg, General Ulysses S. Grant was capturing Vicksburg, Mississippi, cutting off Arkansas and Texas from the rest of the South, and placing the Mississippi River under Union control. Lincoln was convinced that Grant was the leader he needed. When told that Grant had a drinking problem, the president quipped, "Find out what he drinks and I'll send my other generals a case. He fights!" Lincoln promoted Grant to commander of the Union army in March 1864.

Grant and Lincoln planned the campaign they believed could win the war for the Union. Grant attacked on the eastern front, pushing toward Richmond, the rebel capital. By May, General William Tecumseh Sherman was poised at Chattanooga with 100,000 men. His orders were to begin a devastating assault on Georgia. Once Sherman reached the coast, he was to turn north. Lee's forces would be trapped in the middle.

During the spring and summer of 1864, more than 54,000 lives were lost in several major battles in Virginia. Lee's defense stopped Grant, who was unable to capture Richmond. Grant doggedly dug in, saying he would fight all summer if that's what it took. And it did.

Northerners were horrified when they saw reports of the staggering number of casualties. Lincoln, who was facing reelection, was very unpopular, and members of his own party were against him. Yet by June 1864, he had rallied enough support to win the nomination for a second term. By then General William Tecumseh Sherman had captured Atlanta, and suddenly the momentum of the war swung toward the North.

General Ulysses S. Grant. (National Archives and Records Administration)

SHERMAN:
GEN'RAL MOSES

—◁((●))▷—

"The next day we passed through the handsome town of Covington, [Georgia,] the soldiers closing up their ranks, the color-bearers unfurling their flags, and the bands striking up patriotic airs. The white people came out of their houses to behold the sight, 'spite of their deep hatred of the invaders, and the Negroes were simply frantic with joy. Whenever they heard my name, they clustered about my horse, shouted and prayed in their peculiar style, which had a natural eloquence that would have moved a stone. I have witnessed hundreds, if not thousands, of such scenes, and can now see a poor girl, in the very ecstasy of the Methodist 'shout,' hugging the banner of one of the regiments, and jumping up to the 'feet of Jesus.'"

WILLIAM TECUMSEH SHERMAN
Memoirs

1864

FAYETTEVILLE, GEORGIA

Major George E. Nichols is an aide to General William Tecumseh Sherman during his march through Georgia. He has been keeping a record of all the people they have encountered during the campaign.

The army is camped near the town of Fayetteville. As in most of the Georgia towns, all the whites have fled, taking with them all they could pack in a wagon, including the slaves who would go with them.

Most of the slaves are heading west to free territories, but a few slaves, emboldened by the knowledge that the Yankees are coming, remain behind to greet the Deliverer, General Sherman. Among them is an eighty-six-year-old woman with her daughters, their husbands, and their children — numbering fifteen — all of them mulattoes or quadroons. Though they have been warned that the Yankees are mean-spirited dogs, this family is not convinced. The matriarch tells Major Nichols that the family's master offered her sons-in-law freedom if they'd volunteer to fight for the Confederates. "But he should have known better than that," says the woman, a cautious smile brightening her face. "Not me nor mine would fire a gun against the Federals."

Nichols is impressed with the poise and beauty of the daughters. There is no hint of the slave dialect in their language. For all practical purposes they appear to be white, but they are slaves.

One of the young men steps forward. His son proudly stands by his side. "I would not fight for the man who is my master and my father at the same time. If he had forced me into the army, I would have run; I wouldn't have fought."

"Indeed, sir," says the grandmother, "we only want to stay

together as a family. And if we can only get to any place where we can be free and able to work for ourselves, we shall be thankful."

William Tecumseh Sherman, the Deliverer to many slaves. (North Wind Picture Archives)

Many years after the war was over, the mere mention of General William Tecumseh Sherman's name could make the most reverent Southerner swear and spit. In the fall and winter of 1864, enslaved Southerners viewed him as an avenging angel.

Sherman was neither a devil nor a saint, but rather a very good general with a well-equipped, motivated army to do his bidding. Sherman's troops, who affectionately called him "Uncle Billy," admired him because he was a winner. Winning battles meant that the war would come to an end sooner and they could all go home.

Sherman's march through Georgia was intended to bring the South to its knees and leave the rebels with no resources to come back with. Although Sherman had met with fierce resistance, it was not enough to stop the advance, and early in September 1864, Sherman had reached Atlanta, the pearl of the Confederacy. His commanding officer and good friend, General Ulysses S. Grant, who received the news in Washington, D.C., congratulated him, saying, the campaign "was managed with the most consummate skill."

Winning was not enough to stop the rising criticism of Grant's tactics. This was the first war that had been photographed, and when pictures of battle scenes were put on display in New York, people cried out in horror at the sight of young men dead and dying — Union and Confederate. General Grant was accused of using excessive force, and his enemies called for the general's replacement. President Lincoln continued to support Grant and Sherman. They were the best way to end to the war swiftly.

With the president's support, Sherman was ordered to carry on. At the heart of Sherman's campaign was efficiency. His men were to stay light and move fast. In Special Field Order No. 120, dated November 9, 1864, Sherman informed his troops that they would carry no supplies because it would slow them down. They'd have to live off the land as they marched. "The army will forage liberally on the country during the march . . ." Horses, mules, livestock, wagons, and more, could be taken by the cavalry and artillery "freely and without limit." His men were to refrain from abusive or threatening language, and endeavor "to leave with each family a reasonable portion for their maintenance." Regarding blacks, troops were ordered to take along any able-bodied man or woman who could be of service and wanted to leave.

The capture of Atlanta, Georgia, by Union troops. (Hulton/Archive by Getty Images)

With these orders in place, on the morning of November 16, 1865, Sherman's troops mounted their horses and turned toward the rising sun. With the band playing "John Brown's Body," they headed east, toward Savannah, leaving Atlanta burning behind them.

The Confederacy, hearing about the siege of Atlanta, sent the following urgent message, which was printed and distributed:

Richmond, November 18, 1864

To the People of Georgia:

You have now the best opportunity ever yet presented to destroy the enemy. Put everything at the disposal of our generals; remove all provisions from the path of the invader, and put all obstructions in his path.

Every citizen with his gun, and every Negro with his spade and axe, can do the work of a soldier. You can destroy the enemy by retarding his march.

Georgians, be firm! Act promptly, and fear not!

B. H. HILL
Senator

I most cordially approve the above.

JAMES A. SEDDON
Secretary of War

Sherman's push to the sea was met with ineffective opposition. His troops were overwhelming. Seeing them coming, one slave asked, "Are there any folk left in the North?"

Two days after leaving Atlanta, Sherman encountered something he had not expected in all his planning. Taking up the rear were hundreds of slaves. He tried but was unable to persuade them to stay where they were until the war ended. During the day, the "contraband" fell back, but under the cloak of nightfall they gathered just outside camp, their voices rising in song around flickering campfires. Wherever "Gen'ral Sherman" went, they were going, too — 10,000 strong!

Hearing that the Yanks were coming, the Confederates left Savannah, and on the morning of December 21, 1864, Sherman's troops marched into the city, claiming yet another Union victory. Behind them came thousands of newly freed slaves, shouting for joy — "Jubilee," "Jubilee," and "Jubilee." For decades after the war, the black population of Savannah dated events not by clock-time or calendar but by "when Tecumsay [William Tecumseh] was here."

To the freedmen, Lincoln was to be forever "the Emancipator" and Sherman "the Deliverer" — somebody akin to Moses. At first, Sherman seemed almost supernatural to the slaves he had emancipated. But after getting to know him, blacks realized the general was a man. Unlike a lot of well-meaning whites, Sherman spoke openly and respectfully with black people, and he had a way of being courteous without becoming too familiar.

A delegation of Savannah blacks, interviewed by Secretary of War Stanton, said of the general:

> *"Some of us called upon him immediately upon his arrival, and it is probable that he did not meet the secretary with more courtesy than he did us. His conduct and deportment toward us characterized him as a friend and gentleman."*

With Savannah secure, Sherman turned north and marched into South Carolina. Union troops were closing in on the capital city of Charleston. South Carolina was now checkmated.

BLACKS
IN GRAY

⟆⟆⟆⟆

"... Us was Confederates all the while, leastwise I means my mammy and my pappy and me and all the rest of the children, 'cause Old Marse was, and Marse Jeff woulda fit 'em too and me with him iffen we had been old enough."

JAMES GILL
Arkansas
Slave Narrative

1864

HALIFAX, VIRGINIA

(based on a Slave Narrative)

Philip Coleman is one of a hundred slaves who belongs to Bird Rogers, a tobacco planter in Halifax, Virginia. By all accounts Rogers is a decent man with a moderate temper — the head of a "quality" family from a long line of Southern aristocracy.

Coleman, born in 1832, was a field hand until he was selected to be the plantation coachman. Accustomed to being in the company of wealthy men, he prided himself on being a gentleman's gentleman, intolerant himself of riffraff (poor whites).

Coleman was almost thirty when the war started and during it his world was altered forever. His master is, of course, a supporter of the Confederacy. Though there's been no fighting in Halifax, word has come that the Yankees will be arriving soon.

As the Rogers family prepares to aid the rebel army and defend their home, Coleman has no doubt in his mind that the Confederate army will win. He volunteers to fight. But his master forbids him, saying he needs Coleman to stay near the house to protect the women and children should the Yankees break through their lines.

Coleman has no choice but to obey.

But when the Confederate army comes through Halifax, they draft Coleman into service and put him to work digging deep holes in the road and felling trees across the road for the purpose of holding up the Yanks. It does no good. The Union soldiers keep coming.

During combat, Coleman sees white men killed. It amazes him that white men's blood is as red as his own. Coleman also realizes that if these white men can die, so can his master. And that means his master is not invincible as once he'd thought. It is a turning point. Coleman knows now that it makes no sense for him to remain the slave of a man who can bleed and die same as he can. Coleman runs away and never looks back.

Black Union soldiers made a big difference in battles at Port Hudson and Milliken's Bend in Louisiana. They had been at Gettysburg, and had spearheaded the failed assault on Fort Wagner, South Carolina, removing all doubt that black men could be good soldiers. Their successes didn't go unnoticed by Southern leadership. By 1863–64, the slaves who had once been the South's greatest asset were now becoming its greatest liability.

During the early stages of the war, slave men went off to war with the men who owned them, often with the promise that they would be freed for their service. Generals Stonewall Jackson and even Nathan Bedford Forrest had slaves who earned fame for their service and loyalty to their masters.

Stories about "faithful, loyal servants" who stayed with their wounded masters, ran the farms and businesses while the white men were away at war, and protected the family treasures at the risk of their own lives, are abounding. Other stories immortalize blacks who returned wounded or dead Confederate masters to their families. Though these events tend to be exaggerated and romanticized in books and films, there are a few stories that can be verified.

There are, for example, historical markers commemorating Confederate black "soldiers," such as the one at Fort Mill, South Carolina. The inscription is interesting:

> DEDICATED TO THE FAITHFUL SLAVES
>
> WHO LOYAL TO A SACRED TRUST
>
> TOILED FOR THE SUPPORT OF THE ARMY

Most blacks who served the Confederacy were laborers, cooks, or body servants of officers, but toward the end of the war, a few blacks wore gray with distinction.

General Patrick R. Cleburne, a divisional commander of the army of Tennessee, recognized that blacks could be used as soldiers, and he submitted a proposal, on December 18, 1863, recommending the enlistment of slaves. A copy was sent to Jefferson Davis in Richmond, but he immediately rejected the proposal and ordered Cleburne to avoid even the discussion of arming slaves.

Slaves in the Confederate army. (Library of Congress)

But others who saw the merit in using blacks as soldiers refused to drop the discussion. When the idea reached the Confederate congress, many of the same arguments that had kept blacks out of the Union army surfaced: Arming blacks was against Southern traditions; it would offend white soldiers and officers; it would mean the end of slavery; it was too dangerous.

But as the war wore on, many of the plain folk of the South were tired of those excuses. They had become disillusioned and angry, and since they weren't slaveholders, they had no vested interest in preserving the institution. Poor Southerners resented special privileges given to the wealthy and complained that it was "a rich man's war and a poor man's fight" — especially when so many of their sons and husbands, fathers and uncles, were dying in losing battles.

Although Confederate law made all able-bodied men between the ages of eighteen and thirty-five liable for three years' service to the Confederacy, the draft law allowed a draftee to pay a substitute to serve for him (the North adopted a similar law in 1863). Further tension was caused by the "Twenty Negro Law" of October 1862, which exempted one white Southern man from the draft on every plantation with twenty or more slaves. Many young whites fled to the western territories to avoid the Confederate draft and desertions doubled.

General Robert E. Lee desperately needed manpower and the slaves were a logical source. In January 1865, Lee proposed the recruitment of slaves into the Southern military with the promise of freedom to those who served. "I think, therefore, we must decide whether slavery shall be distinguished by our enemies and the slaves used against us," he wrote to the senator from Virginia, "or use them ourselves at the risk of the effects which may be produced on our social system."

The debate was heated in the Confederate Congress, with

several senators promising to fall upon the sword of honor rather than arm slaves. But these were desperate times in the South and with General Lee's endorsement, the "Negro Soldier Law" narrowly passed.

Blacks were quickly recruited in the South — with their masters' approval — helter-skelter and with little or no organization. And there were young white Southerners, such as Walter Clark (who would later become chief justice of South Carolina's supreme court), who chose to be officers in an all-black company rather than remain privates in all-white units.

There was no mad rush of slaves clamoring to join the Confederate army. It was too little, too late. Not even the lure of freedom could bring them out — not in the numbers that were needed. First, not enough of them viewed the Yankees as enemies. Also, slaves could see that the Confederates were losing. Who wanted to join a losing cause — especially a cause that was not in their best interest?

A lot of blacks, however, were cautious and took a "wait-and-see" position. Martin Jackson's father advised him that "the war wasn't going to last forever, but that our forever was going to be spent living among the Southerners after they got licked." Those Southerners, disappointed and embittered by defeat, would still hold tremendous power over their lives. It was wise to be careful when choosing up sides.

Richmond was able to raise two companies of mixed free blacks and slaves. To help recruit others, they were put on exhibition and paraded in their rebel gray, marching in step, spit-polished — a "spectacle to behold," wrote one witness. This was the extent of the "black rebel army."

A week later, Richmond was deserted. The Yanks were coming. Looking at the facts closely, the South never armed a substantial number of blacks to make a difference in combat.

HALLELUJAH BROKE OUT

—⟨(●)⟩—

"These were the Union men going after Lee's army, which had done been 'fore them to Appomattox . . . The colored regiment came up behind, and when they saw the colored regiment they put up the white flag. Well, honey, that white flag was a token that Lee had surrendered. Glory! Glory! Yes, child, the Negroes was free. We began to sing:

> *Run to the kitchen window*
> *Mammy don't you cook no more,*
> *You are free! You are free!*
> *Run to the fence*
> *Rooster don't you crow no more,*
> *You are free! You are free!*
> *Run to the chicken coop*
> *Old hen don't you lay no more,*
> *You are free! You are free!*
> *Run to the front door*
> *Missus don't you call me no more,*
> *I'm free! I'm free!*

Such rejoicing and shouting you never heard before."

Slave Narrative

CANADA

Samuel Gridley Howe, premiere educator of the blind and an abolitionist, had been one of six men who financed John

Brown's insurrection of 1859. He has now come to Canada to interview fugitive slaves. He's spent weeks recording fugitive slave stories — some too cruel to imagine, some reliving the emotional trauma of daring escapes and the difficult experiences of adjusting to a new home in a foreign land. He is physically exhausted and emotionally drained. He longs to be at home again among family and friends. But he feels his work is important.

Howe also interviews J. W. Lindsay, who had escaped from Tennessee in 1838 at the age of twenty. Working as a blacksmith in Canada, he is now a successful businessman. Howe had asked if he had experienced any cruelty while in slavery.

Lindsay answers that in Tennessee he had seen two slaves who were eighty years old or more who had been turned out by their master. "They were old and of no more use, so their master had turned them loose [freed them] upon the mercy of the world." They were near starvation when Lindsay saw them. Filled with compassion, he'd given them a piece of meat. The elderly woman had kissed his hand and blessed him. He can't help but think that his own mother might be in need of a similar kindness one day. Lindsay says that "turning out" is the meanest thing he remembered about slavery. Even now, his eyes still fill with water as he tells the story.

Howe is surprised that a majority of the men and women

living safely in Canada, when asked what they thought about the war, and if they would be willing to fight, answered yes. "I think the North will whip the South, because I believe they are in the right . . . I will return to fight with them, if they want me to." But even more surprising is that almost all of the fugitives say they will return to the United States when the war is over and slavery is totally abolished. "I got family back in Kentucky," says a Canadian fugitive. "I want to see them again."

When Howe returns to Boston, he is expected to make a full report of his findings to the American Freedmen's Inquiry Commission. He plans to report that, among the Canadian fugitives, he has found a thriving, successful, industrious, hard-working, and intelligent community. This image is a contradiction of the shiftless, lazy, and ignorant stereotypes perpetuated by pro-slavery advocates. Howe has seen convincing evidence that if the newly freed men of the South are provided with educational and employment opportunities, they have the ability to become successful and contributing members of society.

Five thousand black infantrymen and 1,800 black cavalrymen, many of them former Virginia slaves, some from as far away as Canada, rode into Richmond in April 1865. Thomas Morris Chester of Ohio was one of those Virginia sons who'd returned as a liberator. Chester said he and others like him had come home to "tear down Jeff Davis's nest." The black soldiers were greeted with shouts of "hosanna to the deliverers."

A day or so later, President Lincoln, accompanied by his son Tad, came to Richmond. He greeted the commanding officers, all the white and black troops, and civilians. He entered the Confederate White House and sat in Jefferson Davis's chair. Then in his own enigmatic style, Lincoln asked for a band to play "Dixie."

For all practical purposes the war was over, but it became official on April 9, 1865, when General Robert E. Lee surrendered to

Lee's surrender to Grant.
(Culver Picture Archive)

General Ulysses S. Grant at the Appomattox Court House in Virginia.

As word of Lee's surrender went out over the wire, celebrations erupted spontaneously. "Grandma dropped her hoe and run to the Thacker place," a former slave who remembered the surrender reported. "She looked at Ole Missus for a long time. 'I'se free! Yes, I'se free! Ain't got to work fo' you no mo'. You can't put me in yo' pocket now!' Missus Thacker started boo-hooing an' threw her apron over her face an' runned in de house."

Freedom meant they could do things and say things they'd been holding in for years. When Tempie Cummins's mother was freed she left the plantation, but she came back for her daughter, who lived in the Big House. Emboldened by freedom, Tempie's mother challenged her former mistress, saying, "You took her away from me an' didn't pay no mind to my cryin', so now I'se takin' her back!"

After generations of being chained to the land, many blacks had no concept of what to do or where to go. Without money, education, jobs, or a place to live, their options were very limited. A former slave from Georgia told an interviewer, "When the war was over and the slaves [were] called up and told they was free, some was glad an' some was sorry. Dey all was at a wonder — didn't know where to go." Jane Johnson from South Carolina said, "I was kinda lonesome and sadlike. Us slaves was lost."

Many were fearful, because they had been provided for in varying degrees of poverty, but now they were free and responsible for themselves. Without ever being allowed off the plantation, they had very little knowledge of the world. Slaves had been forbidden even to pray for freedom, so many of them were fearful about celebrating openly. "We was scared — scared we be foun't out and git a good whuppin'," one slave reported. "We was just like turtles after emancipation. Jes' stick our heads out to see how the land lay," said another.

Some former planters generously divided up their land among their former slaves and either went to Europe or moved out west to start over again. Depending upon the master's need, slaves were invited to stay on and work for wages. Bert Strong of Georgia made that decision. "When the war am over," Strong reported, "[Young Massa] come home and say to Old Massa, 'Ain't you read the proclamation to your slaves yet?' Massa say he hasn't, and Young Massa blowed the horn and calls us all up and tells us we's free as he is and could work for who we please, but he likes us to stay till the crop am out. Me and my mammy stay ten years."

Tenant farming, or "sharecropping," wasn't a new practice. Poor whites often rented small farms from large landowners for a share in the profit. Once the slaves were free, many families joined this system. Their former masters owned the land and they farmed

A family of free sharecroppers after the Civil War. (Cook Collection, Valentine Museum, Richmond, Virginia)

it — same as before. Little had changed. The sharecropping system never really benefited anyone. For one reason, it was never practiced fairly.

While the newly freed people celebrated, Confederate officers and soldiers were returning to their scorched and desolate land. "We are skattered," wrote Mary Chesnut, "stunned; the remnant of heart left alive is filled with brotherly hate . . . Only the dead heroes left stiff and stark on the battlefield escape."

Confederates were returning in no mood to sing or dance. They had two choices: pick up and start rebuilding or continue to resist the new order. Unfortunately, a lot of Southerners chose to resist. The freeing of slaves was not what was most objectionable. It was the "equality" issue they resisted the most. Southerners weren't alone in that objection; plenty of Northerners shared that sentiment.

Losing the war was a very traumatic experience and the planters often vented their anger, fear, and frustration in ways that were cruel and violent. The Freedmen's Bureau reports are filled with complaints that former masters threatened to kill rather than let their slaves leave. One Tennessee man told his slaves at gunpoint, "You free to live and free to die and free to go to the devil. Which will it be?"

A few rebels chose to leave the country rather than accept the outcome of the war. Others commited suicide. For example, Edmund Ruffin of Virginia, who had been the first to fire shots at Fort Sumter in Charleston, South Carolina, wrapped himself in a Confederate flag and shot himself.

Tom Wilson's master was so angry about the outcome of the war, he went "off down to a li'l stream of water an' broke de ice an' jumped in. He died 'bout two weeks afte' of the pneumonia."

To restore either their real or imagined loss of honor, courage, and manhood, Confederate men redefined their cause as one of noble sacrifice. This allowed them to claim an ultimate moral victory. They could not do that unless they maintained the illusion of black inferiority. Thus, there was a rise of white-supremacy groups such as the Ku Klux Klan, organized in Pulaski, Tennessee, by Confederate General Nathan Bedford Forrest. Similar secret and underground organizations formed with the intent to intimidate and impede the progress of blacks and their supporters. These prevailing attitudes among whites are probably what led Reverend Garrison Frazier of the Sea Islands, Georgia, to ask General William T. Sherman to allow blacks to live separate and apart from whites, "[f]or there is a prejudice against us in the South that will take years to get over."

Individual moments of celebration gave way to larger, better-planned affairs — some elaborate, some less so. They were scheduled throughout the year. Often Northern blacks, mostly runaways or antislavery supporters, came south to participate in the festivities. Frederick Douglass went to Nashville and back to Maryland where he'd been a slave.

A reporter who witnessed a parade held by Charleston blacks a month after the surrender of the city on February 17, 1865, gave a detailed description of the event for the New York *Tribune:* "The band led the way. Then came the 21st Black Regiment, stepping proud, then the clergymen of the city followed, carrying open Bibles. Behind them was a long procession of women and children — said to be 1,800 in number — singing joyfully:

We'll hang Jeff Davis on a sour apple tree!

As we go marching on!"

After the children, a group of fishermen marched in, carrying a banner that said THE FISHERMEN WELCOME YOU, GENERAL SAXTON. Next were the craftsmen of the city — carpenters, blacksmiths, masons, teamsters, drovers, coopers, wheelwrights, and barbers.

Coming up behind them was an old cart drawn by a mule. It represented the auction block. A black man with a bell impersonated a slave trader. "I later learned," wrote the reporter, "that this man had himself been sold several times."

Two women were standing in the cart, each holding a child. There commenced a mock auction with the pretend auctioneer calling out: "How much am I offered for this good cook? She is an excellent cook, gentlemen."

It was only a skit, intended to show what blacks did not have to endure any longer. But the memory was too fresh in the minds of the spectators. They openly sobbed. One woman wailed pitifully, as if reliving the scene in reality, "Give me back my children. Give me back my children!"

Mary Chesnut saw the festival in Charleston, too. She wrote about it with contempt:

◆　◆　◆

"Yesterday, there was a mass meeting of [N]egroes, thousands of them were in town, eating, drinking, dancing, speechifying. Preaching and prayer was also a popular amusement. They have no greater idea of amusement than wild prayers — unless it be getting married or going to a funeral."

It wasn't uncommon for the newly freed men and women to stay with their masters until the harvest was over . . . then through the winter . . . then through planting time again. "First thing I knowed," remembered a Virginia woman, "we'd stayed on the place free longer than we'd stayed as slaves."

LINCOLN BELONGS
TO THE AGES

"Look at Lincoln now. How we used to hate him — abuse him. And now who is so base as to utter a word against the murdered president?"

MARY CHESNUT

1865

Alexander Gardner, a photographer, is developing a photograph of Abraham Lincoln early in the spring of 1865. The plate cracks and he has to discard it after making only one print. "Oh, well," he sighs, "there will be plenty of time for me to get another shot." Little does Gardner know that Lincoln has less than a month to live.

Elizabeth Keckley mentions to Mrs. Lincoln that while the president was speaking the evening before, he was totally exposed. The president could be targeted by an assassin. "What an easy matter would it be to kill the president, as he stands there!" says Mrs. Keckley. "He could be shot from the crowd, and no one would be able to tell who fired the shot."

Mrs. Lincoln seems more agitated than usual. She replies

with a deep sigh, "Yes, yes, Mr. Lincoln's life is always exposed."
Then fighting off the terrible feeling of doom, the First Lady
adds, "Ah, no one knows what it is to live in constant dread of
some fearful tragedy. The president has been warned so often
that I tremble for him on every public occasion. I have a pre-
sentiment that he will meet with a sudden and violent end."

They have no way of knowing that in reality the president
will be dead in a few days.

General and Mrs. Grant are invited to attend a play with
the president and First Lady, but at the last minute, the Grants
cancel and leave for Philadelphia. Within hours, the president
will be shot while attending that play.

Omens?

Who knows?

But on Friday, April 14, 1865, John Wilkes Booth mur-
ders President Abraham Lincoln at Ford's Theatre in
Washington, D.C.

Lincoln was reelected on November 8, 1864, defeating General
George McClellan and General John C. Frémont. McClellan had
campaigned that he would end the war, and restore the Union and
slavery. Frémont campaigned on a third-party ticket, promising that
he would end the war with a Northern victory and that he would

deal with the South harshly. Lincoln won by a half-million votes.

President Lincoln's second inaugural speech was strikingly different in tone and content from his first. This time the president clearly stated that slavery was an evil practice. While campaigning, Lincoln had worked with Senator Charles Sumner and Representative Thaddeus Stevens on drafting a Thirteenth Amendment to the Constitution — abolishing slavery forever. The final vote in the House of Representatives came on January 31, 1865. Lincoln proclaimed that it was a "great moral victory."

On April 14, 1865, a few days after the surrender at Appomattox, the Lincolns went to Ford's Theatre to see a light comedy, *Our American Cousin.*

Lincoln was in great spirits that evening. The guard who was supposed to have secured the door to the Lincolns' box became so engrossed in the drama, that he didn't notice John Wilkes Booth, an actor, step inside. At point-blank range, Booth shot President

The death of President Lincoln. (The Harry T. Peters Collection, Museum of the City of New York)

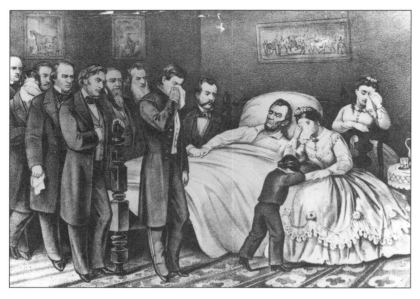

Lincoln in the back of the head. The bullet passed through his brain and lodged behind his right eye. Yelling, *"Sic semper tyrannis* [thus be it ever to tyrants]," Booth leaped onto the stage, injuring his leg in the process, but he was still able to escape.

President Lincoln died at 7:22 A.M., April 15, 1865, in a boardinghouse across the street from the theater. He was fifty-six years old. Secretary of War Edwin Stanton who was there whispered, "Now he belongs to the ages."

After hearing about the president's death, Frederick Douglass gathered with others at City Hall in Rochester, New York. Douglass and Lincoln had differed greatly on issues such as colonization, blacks' fitness to serve in the military, and compensated emancipation. Still, Douglass had grown to admire the president, because Lincoln had the courage to change his mind.

Although Douglass was not scheduled to speak at City Hall, he was called upon to say a few words. He delivered an impassioned eulogy, with choked emotion:

"Viewed from the genuine abolition ground, Mr. Lincoln seemed tardy, cold, dull, and indifferent: But measuring him by the sentiment he was bound as a statesman to consult, he was swift, zealous, radical, and determined . . . But by dying as he did die, by the red hand of violence . . . taken off without warning . . . he is doubly dear to us, and his memory will be precious forever . . ."

Even though the Emancipation Proclamation had not freed many slaves, it held great political significance to the former slaves. And when the author of that proclamation was killed, the freed men and women experienced it as a personal loss. They were fearful that they might be reenslaved. For most blacks, Abraham Lincoln, though he was a reluctant emancipator, would be forever associated with the "freeing of the slaves."

Lincoln's body lay in state, first at the White House. Mary Lincoln was so distraught, she could not move from her bed, permitting only her sons, Elizabeth Keckley, and several cabinet wives to see her. Keckley remembered the effect Mrs. Lincoln's grief had on Tad: "Sometimes he would throw his arms around her neck, and exclaim, between his broken sobs, 'Don't cry so, Mamma! Don't cry, or you will make me cry, too! You will break my heart . . .' Mrs. Lincoln could not bear to hear Tad cry, and when he would plead to her not to break his heart, she would calm herself with a great effort, and clasp her child in her arms."

Mrs. Lincoln was positive that Jefferson Davis and other Confederates were the real assassins. Her accusations were not without support. Edwin Stanton and newly sworn-in President Andrew Johnson also believed that Lincoln had been murdered by orders from Confederate leaders. Investigations were under way even as Lincoln lay in state in the White House.

The 22nd Regiment of African American troops took positions along Pennsylvania Avenue as the president's funeral procession moved from the White House to the Capitol. The funeral train took fourteen days to travel 1,662 miles back to Springfield, Illinois, where the president and the exhumed body of his son Willie would be buried.

All along the way, people came to pay their respects. Americans of every sex, age, and race lined the railroad tracks as the funeral train passed. From city to city, station to station, the black-draped train stopped for public viewing of the body. Over mountains, through valleys, and into the Great Plains, the train inched along. Black mourners waved good-bye, openly wailing, moaning, and crying. They would not be comforted.

At last the funeral car arrived in Springfield on May 4, 1865. There, friends and neighbors walked past the coffin that held the country lawyer who had become president. He'd come home to rest. In the dull light of a gentle spring rain, thousands of people watched in silence as the caskets of Lincoln and his beloved son Willie were placed in a vault at Oak Ridge Cemetery.

Lincoln was the first president to be assassinated in office, and the nation demanded justice. On April 26, Booth and coconspirator David Herold were captured in a Virginia tobacco barn. Booth refused to surrender, so the barn was set on fire. When he fled the flames, Booth was shot in the head by Sergeant Boston Corbett.

Hundreds of people were detained and questioned throughout the South. Seven men and one woman were captured and hastily tried before a military commission. All eight were found guilty. Edman Spangler, the man who held Booth's horse behind Ford's Theatre the night of the assassination, was given eight years (some sources say six

John Wilkes Booth.
(Corbis Images)

President Lincoln's private box at Ford's Theatre. (Library of Congress)

years). Three received life sentences, including Dr. Samuel Mudd, who treated Booth's broken leg. Mudd swore his innocence, claiming that he had no idea Booth was an assassin. He was sent to Fort Jefferson on Dry Tortugas in Key West, Florida. During a yellow-fever epidemic, Dr. Mudd helped treat both prisoners and guards. He was given a pardon in 1868. But his name became synonymous with a defamed character and gave rise to the adage, "your name will be Mudd."

The last four conspirators were hanged on July 7. It was an oppressively hot day in Washington in the arsenal grounds of the Old Penitentiary building, where a large crowd had gathered. Lewis Payne, George A. Azerodt, David Herold, and Mrs. Mary E. Surratt were pronounced guilty of their crime. There was hope that perhaps the president might show mercy to Mary since she was a woman. But she was hanged along with the rest, even though she maintained her innocence, as did the other assassins.

Without Lincoln, the question then was: How would the millions of African Americans be incorporated into a restructured nation where slavery no longer existed? These and other questions were on the minds of the new leaders and the freedmen.

FREEDOM DON'T MAKE YOU RICH

"We knowed freedom was on us, but we didn' know what was to come with it. We thought we was going to get rich like the white folks. We thought we was going to be richer than the white folks, 'cause we was stronger and knowed how to work, and the whites didn't, and they didn't have us to work for them anymore. But it didn't turn out that way. We soon found out that freedom could make folks proud, but it didn't make them rich."

> *FRANK PATTERSON*
> *North Carolina*
> *Slave Narrative*

1865

MISSISSIPPI

Lucretia Alexander cups her hand over her eyes and looks toward the Big House. The plantation bell is ringing and that can mean only one thing — something important has happened or is getting ready to happen. There has been talk in the Quarters that the war will soon be over. Lucretia hasn't heard the sounds of cannon fire in the distance or the echo of men's voices rising off the river mists in a long while. So she guessed that the Yankees weren't coming.

Ol' Marse has been more sour than ever, since they'd brought home a second son to bury. The baby boy was not yet eighteen. "Two sons is too much for any family to sacrifice," he'd yelled, weeping bitterly over the grave. Then Ol' Marse had turned his anger on his slaves as if they'd had something to do with it. Lucretia figured the bell wasn't ringing for another son, because Ol' Marse didn't have another son to offer.

What can it be then?

As the field hands head for the house, they see one of the house slaves is running to meet them, waving his hands.

"Who rang the bell?" Mama Della asks.

"I did," the slave answers. "A man named Captain Barkus, whose arm is off at the elbow, is calling for all of us from three plantations to meet here at our place. He's got something to tell us!"

At the Big House, Missus and Ol' Marse are standing on the porch, watching without saying a word. About that time, Captain Barkus stands up on the back of the wagon. Another man stands beside him. "This is Mr. Loggins, an agent of the Freedmen's Bureau, and he has come to tell you something very important," says Captain Barkus.

Mr. Loggins clears his throat and declares that the war is over. There is peace and all slaves are free. This is the first time Lucretia hears the word that she's free and that the war is over.

> *"The war is over! You've been free for a long time, but you were not told,"* says Mr. Loggins, casting an accusing eye toward Missus and Ol' Marse. *"Nobody can keep you now against your own free will."* Then the agent points to a colored man and yells, *"You are free as I am."*
>
> It takes a moment, but when the idea soaks in, Granny, who has been walking on a stick, throws it away and shouts for joy. But Lucretia quietly reflects on the idea that she is free — even though she is getting the news late, she is free nonetheless. It takes a long while for her to really believe it. *"Bless the Freedmen's Bureau,"* she whispers. Then she drops her hoe and walks away never looking back . . . not once.

News of the Appomattax surrender was slow reaching the West. As last as May 13, 1865, the 62nd U.S. Colored Infantry was still engaged in battle with Texas Confederates. A black sergeant by the name of Crocket was the last casualty of the Civil War, black or white, Confederate or Union.

And throughout 1865 there were still thousands of black people who remained in bondage.

They belonged to masters who either kept the news of freedom hidden or forced them to stay at gunpoint. During an interview, Will Sheet said that when his mistress announced that all slaves were free, "Marse Jeff said us wasn't, and he didn't tell us no different 'til 'bout Christmas after the war was done over with in April."

One of the first responsibilities of Freedmen's Bureau agents was to go throughout the South and tell the slaves they were free. Edna Harper from Mississippi said a government worker emancipated her. "When the war ended, a white man come to the field and tells my mother-in-law we free as he is. She dropped her hoe and danced up to the turn road and danced right up into Old Marser's parlor. That was in June [1865]."

The eighth of May, 1865 (pronounced "Eighta-May"), was celebrated as a day of Jubilee, because that's when Mississippi and Louisiana slaves finally got word that the war was over and they were free. In Florida, May 20 was celebrated. In the Alabama towns of Eufaula and Rutherford and neighboring Georgia counties, the freedmen held "drum-dancing" to remember their May 28 "Emancipation Day." Reverend Thomas J. Flanagan of Thomaston, Georgia, reported in an interview that the celebrants "would beat that drum and barbecue goats and have a big time."

A common practice among Southerners was "refugeeing" with their slaves and other possessions, to avoid emancipation and Union confiscation. Countries such as Brazil and Cuba offered safe havens for slaveholders, too. In those countries slavery lasted for another forty years after it had ended in the United States. Texas was also a favorite location to refugee. "In Texas dere never be no freedom," recalled William Mathews of Georgia, whose master had moved his family and slaves there early on in the war.

The news of freedom didn't reach Texas until June 19, 1865, when Major General Gordon Granger arrived in Galveston and announced that all slaves were emancipated, two and a half years after Lincoln's Proclamation had been signed. The date, known as "Juneteenth," is one of the few surviving Jubilee holidays still celebrated in the country.

Later dates of emancipation were recorded by the Freedmen's Bureau agents. For example, Willie Stone said, "I hears 'bout freedom in September [1865], when a government agent rode up to the farm and told us we was free."

Aside from making people aware that they were free, the Freedmen's Bureau was charged with the responsibility of expanding the works of private and religious organizations, which had come to the South to offer relief to millions of people. The bureau was also responsible for passing and enforcing regulations that safeguarded the rights of the newly freed.

The bureau opened offices throughout the South and officials took complaints from former slaves who were victimized by their former owners. They negotiated with white leaders and tried to resolve commu-

Union officer standing as peacemaker between opponents of the Freedmen's Bureau program.
(Brown Brothers)

nity conflicts among blacks. But resources were limited, and some of the agents were of questionable character. Unfortunately, the agency was often judged by its critics, on the basis of the misdeeds of a few rather than on the successes of the many. The agents and other Northern whites who came South to help during Reconstruction were generally lumped together in a term called "carpetbaggers."

Reuniting families was something good agents took pride in achieving. They assisted by writing letters and making inquiries. Asking newspapers to print information was a method of tracing the whereabouts of loved ones, too:

To the Editor:

I have a mother somewhere in the world. I know not where. She used to belong to Philip Mathias in Elbert County, Georgia, and she left four of her children there about twenty-three years ago and I have never heard of her since. I ask all who read this to inquire for her. Her name was Martha and I heard that she was carried off to Mississippi by speculators. If any of you can give me information about her it will be gladly received. I am a member of the [Methodist] M.E. Church.

REVEREND E. W. JOHNSON

St. Louis, Missouri

Colored citizen

To protect families, the bureau passed a regulation stating that parents were in charge of their minor children, except in the case of orphans. If no one claimed former slave children, then they could become wards of their former masters until age twenty-one. Subverting this regulation, some whites told black families that the government had said they could keep their children until maturity. This was a common abuse and some black children remained in a slavelike condition long after the Thirteenth Amendment was passed, ending slavery in the United States of America.

Slave conditions were awful by normal standards. But the slaves' general sense of normalcy was different. Many of them lived in miserable conditions, but they lived miserably as slaves. The difference was that now they were free. With no money, poor shelter, not enough food, no education, and no jobs, Lewis Bonner of Texas spoke for many when he said, "I was in bad shape when freedom come. Aine got much now, but it's mine. I earned every bit of this little somethin' I got, and can't nobody come take it 'cause I got papers on it." A freedman from Georgia expressed a similar sentiment when he told an interviewer: "Slavery was bad, and freedom aine been much better, but I aine a slave. That means I aine got to be down always."

Freedom meant different things to different people and they responded accordingly. For one woman, naming her child without her master's permission was an act of freedom. Others felt freedom meant they could go wherever they wanted, whenever they wanted. Large groups of the freed migrated west and many men became cowboys, or signed on as Pullman car porters when the

An American Pullman sleeping car. (Hulton/Archive by Getty Images)

Transcontinental Railroad was completed. Others established small black farming communities that prospered and grew. Going to sea was the greatest form of escape. "I went to sea after freedom," said a black sailor, "and I get restless whenever we're in port too long."

But for every former slave who left, a thousand stayed in the South. The day-to-day harshness of their lives settled in as the days of Jubilee came to an end. Patsy Moore from Mississippi remembered what it was like after the celebrations ended. "When freedom come, folks left home, out in the streets, crying, praying, singing, shouting, yelling, and knocking down everything. Some shot off big guns. Then come the calm. It was sad then. So many folks done dead [sic], things tore up, and nowheres to go and nothing to eat, nothing to do . . . Folks got sick, so hungry. Some folks starved nearly to death. Times got hard . . ."

At the end of the war 600,000 troops were dead, thousands more were wounded, and many more thousands had died of cholera, infections, and other diseases. Times were hard and bound to get harder.

Slaves had made their masters rich by farming their land, so blacks understood that their freedom was tied to land ownership. Why not farm for themselves and prosper? "Give us a little piece of land — four to five acres — and we can build a house and call it a home," said one Mississippi freedman. A South Carolina freedman told a government agent, "Give us our own land and we can take care of ourselves."

General William Tecumseh Sherman agreed with this concept, and had divided up the Sea Islands among the freed people, deeding forty acres to each family.

Agents of the Freedmen's Bureau with freed slaves on Sea Islands, Georgia. (Massachusetts Commandery Military Order of the Loyal Legion and the U.S. Army Military History Institute)

Thaddeus Stevens introduced a bill in Congress, calling for a similar program to be instituted on a national basis. According to this plan, each former slave family would have been given forty acres of confiscated land. But the bill never passed.

Frederick Douglass wrote: "When you turned us loose you gave us no acres; you turned us loose to the sky, to the storm, to the whirlwind, and, worst of all, you turned us loose to the wrath of our infuriated masters."

"We got free in Georgia, June 15, 1865. I'll never forget that date. What I mean is, that was the day the big freedom came. But we didn't know it and just worked on."

Henry Miller

Georgia

NO MORE
SLAVERY — EVER

—►◄((●))►◄—

"My little boy asked me what the man meant when he say we was emancipated. I tells him we don't belong to nobody. We can come and go as we please, and can't nobody take him away from me. We aine slaves no more. Then he looked at me in the face and say, 'There's no more slavery — ever?' I says, 'No more slavery — ever.'"

Arkansas, 1865
Slave Narrative

MAY 24, 1865

WASHINGTON, D.C.

The flag is flying at full staff above the White House again, the first time since President Lincoln's death. The new president, Andrew Johnson, and General Ulysses S. Grant watch as 150,000 officers and soldiers of the Grand Armies of the Republic parade past. Drums beating. Bands playing. Schoolchildren line the street — singing and cheering. The waving of handheld flags is like thousands of excited butterflies flapping their wings in a frenzied ballet of joy.

General William T. Sherman is concerned that his men will not make a proper showing because they are sunburned, lean, and somewhat shabbily dressed compared to the other units. They are weary. Some of them are sick — of mind and body. They have seen too much. They long to go home.

All night General Sherman is fearful they will be measured by their appearance and not as the brave men he has come to know and respect. Survivors all.

But now it is morning. Nine o'clock sharp. No time to fret any longer. Mounted at the front of the troops, Sherman spurs his horse at the first sound of "The Star-Spangled Banner." The crowd bursts into deafening cheers and shouts of praise as Sherman and his men parade in triumph. No need to worry any longer. The crowd doesn't care about how they look.

Those cheering the loudest are African American troops, who over his objections, were not allowed to march in the parade. Their outpouring of gratitude is expressed in the removal of hats, the waving of handkerchiefs, and the bows of respect as Gen'ral Moses passes.

The two-day victory parade in Washington, D.C., was a clear indication of what blacks might expect for the "reunified" America. No black military units were allowed to participate, and even black spectators were discouraged from attending the celebration.

Instead they were told to wait or to hold their "own" parades. But even more hurtful were the few blacks allowed in the Grand parade, who were made to look foolish and inept. Of course the spectacle of grown men riding small mules and carrying picks and shovels drew laughter, it was not funny to the black soldiers who had fought and died for freedom.

Although it didn't appear so at the time, progress was being made that would benefit the freedmen and their grandchildren and great-grandchildren a century later.

The Thirteenth Amendment was passed by the House of Representatives before President Lincoln died, on January 31, 1865, by a margin of 119 to 56. By then, several slave states — Arkansas, Louisiana, Maryland, Missouri, and Tennessee — already had begun ratifying new constitutions that abolished slavery, anyway. That caused the states' rights issue to surface again. Should each state abolish slavery or should the Constitution be amended? To be rid of slavery forever Senators Charles Sumner and Lyman Trumbull and Representative Thaddeus Stevens pushed for immediate ratification by the states. Otherwise, they believed, slavery might — at a later date — be reestablished whenever a state wanted to do so.

The Fifteenth Amendment.
(Library of Congress)

Ratification of the Thirteenth Amendment by the states was completed December 18, 1865. Actually, this is the true Emancipation Day — the long-awaited Day of Jubilee, but the day passed unnoticed by most blacks. They clung to the idea that their freedom was a debt owed to President Lincoln's January 1, 1863, Emancipation Proclamation. Nothing could change that idea.

Meanwhile, between 1866 and 1870 Sumner and Stevens and other Republican leaders pushed through the Fourteenth and Fifteenth Amendments to the Constitution. The Fourteenth Amendment granted blacks the citizenship they had been denied by the Supreme Court's Dred Scott decision of 1857. The amendment also guaranteed blacks the right to due process of law, and forbade a state from passing a law in conflict with the U.S. Constitution. The Fifteenth Amendment gave men the right to vote regardless of race, religion, or position of servitude. With the three "Reconstruction" amendments in place, it was believed that African American civil rights finally were protected — or so it seemed. But on the issue of justice and equal rights, black people had a much longer and much more difficult battle to fight.

In the meantime, the nation began the slow process of healing. At less than twenty-five years of age, Colonel Elisha Hunt Rhodes beat the odds by surviving the war. Returning to Providence, Rhode Island, he became a successful businessman in the cotton and wool industry. His Civil War diary was published and remains in print today.

Mary Chesnut's world was changed completely. She and her

husband, James, returned to Mulberry Plantation outside Charleston, which Union soldiers had sacked and burned. Ironically, Chesnut earned money by selling eggs and butter in partnership with one of her former slaves. She also published her diary.

Jefferson Davis was captured and served two years in prison, after which he spent the rest of his life writing his memoirs. He died in 1889, never feeling that he had been wrong in his actions.

Nathan Bedford Forrest tried promoting railroads unsuccessfully. But, he is most remembered for organizing the Ku Klux Klan in 1867, and serving as its first Imperial Wizard. During the postwar years, the Klan ushered in a period of fear and intimidation directed at the freedmen, their families, and anybody who tried to help them. Cross burnings advanced to home, school, and business burnings, and finally to beatings and lynchings. The Klan became so violent, even Forrest resigned rather than take part. But the monster he had created was impossible to control.

In the early years, the former slaves often responded to terrorism with their own violence. In Louisiana, Alabama, Kentucky, and other states, former slaves armed themselves and fought Klansmen who threatened them. "Them Ku Kluxers were around since before the war," remembered one Georgia former slave during an interview. "At that time they was mostly youngsters full of themselves. After the war, they turned sour. Didn't want us [the freedmen] to have nothing."

Frederick Douglass continued fighting for justice and equal

rights until his death in 1896. He served as ambassador to Haiti and held several other political appointments in Republican administrations. General George McClellan spent time in Europe after losing the 1864 election and later was elected governor of New Jersey. Soldiers on both sides — white and black — reunited in their efforts to defeat the Indians in western lands. Among them were the well-known African American Buffalo Soldiers and William T. Sherman.

General Robert E. Lee swore allegiance to the United States and accepted the presidency of Washington College, a small school in Lexington, Virginia. He died in 1870 of a heart attack, never

President Grant with his wife, family, and friends at Mt. McGregor, New York. (Illinois State Historical Library)

returning to his home in Arlington, Virginia. His land and property became Arlington Cemetery.

General Ulysses S. Grant was elected president of the United States and governed from 1868 to 1876 — a period called Reconstruction. Though he personally advocated civil rights for blacks, the nation was steadily growing weary of the race issue. By the 1880s, the South had begun passing segregation laws that restricted the civil rights of blacks, and the Supreme Court was declaring these state laws constitutional.

Freedom had been a long time coming for three to four million black men, women, and children. Although times were difficult and racism and discrimination were being legalized, they placed their hope in the next generation, those "born free."

"[These children] can be anything they wanted to be because they had never felt the lash," said a former slave woman, admiring her freeborn child. This mother and thousands like her were often too intimidated to enjoy the Fourteenth and Fifteenth Amendments that Sumner and Stevens worked hard to place in the Constitution. It was as if Sumner and Stevens knew that there would come a time when the sons and daughters of former slaves would be engaged in another struggle for justice, but with the Constitution on their side, they would eventually be victorious. That day came when the great-grandchildren of former slaves used the Fourteenth and Fifteenth Amendments to claim a new day of Jubilee during the civil rights movement of the 1960s. The Civil Rights Act of 1964 and the Voting Rights Act of 1965 were signed into law by President Lyndon B. Johnson, a Texan, guaranteeing that all Americans were free and equal under the law.

But freedom is more than just a high-sounding word on paper. Equality cannot remain an idea and be effective. Jubilee should never be a celebration without meaning. Freedom must be constantly reinforced by equality, justice, and peace so that the words of a newly freed child will be true in law and spirit: "There is no more slavery — ever." Jubilee!

THIRTEENTH AMENDMENT TO THE CONSTITUTION

Article XIII

Sec. 1. Neither slavery nor involuntary servitude, except as a punishment for crime whereof the party shall have been duly convicted, shall exist within the United States, or any place subject to their jurisdiction.

Sec. 2. Congress shall have power to enforce this article by appropriate legislation.

Ratified by 27 states

December 18, 1865

TIME LINE

—◦«(◦)»◦—

1860 | Four million blacks are enslaved in the South.

NOVEMBER

4TH: Abraham Lincoln is elected president.

DECEMBER

4TH: South Carolina becomes the first state to secede from the Union, followed by Mississippi, Florida, Alabama, Georgia, and Louisiana. Eventually, Texas, Arkansas, Tennessee, Virginia, and North Carolina will join the rebel states and form the Confederate States of America. Missouri, Maryland, Kentucky, and Delaware are (border) slave states that remain in the Union.

1861 | ### FEBRUARY

4TH: Representatives meet in Alabama to form the Confederate States of America. Jefferson Davis is elected provisional president.

MARCH

4TH: President Abraham Lincoln is inaugurated.

APRIL

12TH: Fort Sumter is attacked in Charleston Harbor.

MAY

15TH: President Lincoln calls for troops to help put down the rebellion. African Americans are not accepted in the military.

24TH: General Benjamin Butler declares fugitive slaves "contraband of war" and puts them to work for the Union.

JULY

21ST: The Confederates score a victory at Bull Run (First Manassas) in Virginia.

AUGUST

6TH: Congress passes the first Confiscation Act, which frees all slaves who are being used in the Confederate war effort.

30TH: Major General John C. Frémont declares martial law in Missouri and frees all the slaves belonging to disloyal slaveholders. President Lincoln orders him to rescind the order in September.

APRIL

1862

3RD: General David Hunter, commander of troops in the South Carolina Sea Islands, forms the first black regiments made up of former slaves. The War Department declines to arm them.

4TH: At the president's request, Congress pledges financial aid to any state agreeing to gradual emancipation that compensates slaveholders whose slaves are freed.

16TH: Congress abolishes slavery in the District of Columbia, with compensation to slaveholders. Congress also appropriates funds for the colonization of freed blacks to Africa, Brazil, or the Caribbean Islands.

MAY

9TH: General David Hunter declares all slaves living in South Carolina, Georgia, and Florida free.

19TH: President Lincoln issues a proclamation nullifying Hunter's emancipation, and he urges the border states to accept gradual emancipation with compensation.

JUNE

19TH: Congress prohibits slavery in U.S. western territories.

JULY

8TH: Lincoln shares the idea of emancipation with his cabinet. It is suggested that he wait for a military victory before releasing it.

AUGUST

22ND: Under General Benjamin Butler, the first African American regiment is officially mustered into the U.S. Army.

28TH: Second Battle of Bull Run.

SEPTEMBER

22ND: Lincoln shares the preliminary Emancipation Proclamation with his cabinet and the country — to become effective January 1, 1863. This version of the document reiterates support for the colonization of freed slaves outside the United States.

JANUARY

1863

1ST: The Emancipation Proclamation is signed by President Lincoln, declaring free all slaves in the Confederate states (except Tennessee, southern Louisiana, and part of Virginia [now West Virginia]) and accepts blacks in the military.

MARCH

16TH: The American Freedmen's Inquiry Commission is appointed by the War Department to investigate the needs of former slaves and how to help them adjust to freedom.

MAY

22ND: The Bureau of Colored Troops is created by the War Department. Black soldiers' pay is less than whites'.

27TH: Black soldiers repel a Confederate advance at Milliken's Bend, Louisiana.

JULY

1ST–3RD: Battle of Gettysburg.

5TH: The Union scores a victory at Vicksburg, Mississippi. Hundreds of slaves are freed by military action.

8TH: President Lincoln selects General Ulysses S. Grant to be the commander to head the Union army.

18TH: Black soldiers spearhead a failed assault on Fort Wagner, South Carolina.

OCTOBER

2ND: The War Department orders full-scale recruitment of black soldiers in Maryland, Missouri, and Tennessee, with compensation to loyal owners.

1864

APRIL

8TH: The Senate approves a constitutional amendment that abolishes slavery.

Fort Pillow Massacre in Tennessee.

JUNE

15TH: The House of Representatives fails to approve a constitutional amendment abolishing slavery.

Congress makes the pay of black soldiers equal to that of white soldiers.

NOVEMBER

8TH: Abraham Lincoln is reelected president, defeating

Democratic candidate, George B. McClellan, and third-party candidate, John C. Frémont.

JANUARY

16TH: General William T. Sherman issues Special Field Order No. 15, setting aside forty acres in parts of coastal South Carolina, Georgia, and Florida to be deeded to former slaves.

31ST: The Thirteenth Amendment passes the House and Senate and is sent to the states to ratify.

MARCH

3RD: Congress establishes the Freedmen's Bureau.

13TH: Confederate Congress passes bill that allows slaves to serve in Confederate army, with permission of their owners.

APRIL

9TH: General Robert E. Lee surrenders. The war is over.

14TH: President Lincoln is assassinated.

MAY

8TH: Blacks in several Mississippi counties learn they are free.

JUNE

19TH: Slaves are emancipated by Union military in Texas. Celebration called "Juneteenth."

DECEMBER

18TH: The Thirteenth Amendment to the U.S. Constitution is ratified; slavery is abolished in the United States.

BIBLIOGRAPHY

BENNETT, LERONE. *Forced into Glory: Abraham's Lincoln's White Dream.* Chicago: Johnson Publishing, 2000.

BERLIN, IRA, BARBARA J. FIELDS, STEVEN MILLER, JOSEPH P. REIDY, AND LESLIE S. ROWLAND, EDS. *Free at Last: A Documentary History of Slavery, Freedom, and the Civil War.* New York: The New Press, 1992.

BRINKLEY, DOUGLAS. *Witness to America.* San Francisco: HarperCollins, 1999.

CLINTON, CATHERINE. *Tara Revisited.* Paris: Abbeville Press, 1952.

DAVIS, CHARLES T., AND HENRY LOUIS GATES. *The Slave's Narrative.* Oxford: Oxford University Press, 1985.

ESCOTT, PAUL. *Slavery Remembered.* Chapel Hill: University of North Carolina Press, 1979.

FISHER, MARK. *Negro Slave Songs in the United States.* New York: Carol Publishing Group, 1953.

FRANKLIN, JOHN HOPE, AND ALFREDA MOSS. *From Slavery to Freedom.* New York: Knopf, 1994.

FREEDMAN, RUSSELL. *Lincoln: A Photobiography.* New York: Houghton Mifflin, 1987.

GLADSTONE, WILLIAM. *The United States Colored Troops.* Gettysburg: Thomas Publications, 1990.

GRANT, ULYSSES. *Personal Memoirs of Ulysses Grant.* New York: Penguin, 1999.

HORTON, OLIVER. *Hard Road to Freedom.* New Jersey: Rutgers University Press, 2000.

HOWELL, DONNA WYANT. *I Was a Slave.* Washington, D.C.: American Legacy Books, 1999.

————. *I Was a Slave: Description of Plantation Life.* Washington, D.C.: American Legacy Books, 1995.

————. *I Was a Slave: Lives of Slave Men.* Washington, D.C.: American Legacy Books, 1995.

HURMENCE, BELINDA, ED. *Before Freedom, When I Just Can Remember.* Winston-Salem, N.C.: John F. Blair, 1989.

JACOBSON, TIM. *Heritage of the South.* New York: Crescent Books, 1992.

KATZ, LOREN. *Eyewitness: A Living Documentary of African-American Contributions to American History.* New York: Ethic, 1995.

KUNHARDT, PHILLIP. *Lincoln: A Biography.* New York: Random House, 1992.

LOWANCE, MASON, ED. *Against Slavery.* Toronto: Penguin Books, 2000.

MCFEELY, WILLIAM. *Frederick Douglass.* London: Norton and Company, 1991.

NASH, GARY, ED. *The American People.* San Francisco: Harper and Row Publishers, 1986.

QUARLES, BENJAMIN. *The Negro in the Civil War.* New York: Little, Brown and Company, 1953.

ROLLINS, RICHARD, ED. *Black Southerners in Gray.* Redondo Beach, CA: Rank and File Publications, 1997.

SHERMAN, WILLIAM. *William Sherman's Memoirs.* New York: Penguin Books, 2000.

STAROBIN, ROBERT. *Blacks in Bondage.* New York: Markus Publishing, 1988.

STERLING, DOROTHY. *We Are Your Sisters.* New York: Norton, 1997.

TRUDEAU, NOAH. *Like Men of War.* Boston: Little, Brown and Company, 1998.

VANDIVER, FRANK. *1001 Things Everyone Should Know About the Civil War.* London: Doubleday, 1999.

WAUGH, CHARLES, AND MARTIN GREENBERG. *The Women's War in the South.* Nashville: Cumberland House, 1999.

WOODWARD, C. VANN, ED. *Mary Chesnut's Civil War.* New Haven, CT: Yale University Press, 1981.

————. *The Private Mary Chesnut.* Oxford: Oxford University Press, 1984.

INDEX

Greenhow, Rose O'Neal, 24

H

Hamlin, Hannibal, 47
Harper's Ferry raid, 12
Hill, Senator B. H., 78–79
Howe, Julia Ward, 31
Howe, Samuel Gridley, 88–90
Hunter, David, 34, 48

J

Jackson, Thomas J. ("Stonewall Jackson"),
    25, 83
Jefferson, Thomas, 2, 5
Johnson, Andrew, 114
Johnson, Lyndon B., 121
Jones, Reverend Absalom, 5, 6
Jubilee day, 4–5, 108, 112, 120–121
    Charleston, South Carolina, 95–96
Juneteenth, 109
    Sherman's march, 80
    Thirteenth Amendment, 117
    Union army and, 33
    Washington, D.C., 38–39
Juneteenth, Jubilee day, 109

K

Kansas-Nebraska Act of 1854, 11
Keckley, Elizabeth, 36–38, 39–40, 42,
    98
Ku Klux Klan, 95, 118

L

Lee, Robert E., 70, 119–120
    Gettysburg, Battle of, 70, 71
    slaves in Confederate army, 85, 86
    surrender of, 88, 91–92, 107
Lewis, Cudjoe, 6–7
Lincoln, Abraham, 9, 13, 15, 41–43, 44,
    45, 99–100
    African American soldiers, 63
    assassination of, 98–100, 101–104, 114

Bull Run, 26–27
    emancipation and, ix, 33, 35, 43, 80
    Emancipation Proclamation, 46–48,
        51–54, 58, 117
    Fort Sumter and, 20
    freedmen and, 40
    Gettysburg, Battle of, 71
    Gettysburg Address, 72
    secession and, 16, 17
    slavery and, 12, 16, 33–34
    Union army, 21, 24, 70, 72–73, 77
Lincoln, Mary Todd, 36–38, 40, 98–99
Lincoln, Tad, 41, 91
Lincoln, Willie, death of, 41–42, 103
Lindsay, J. W., 89

M

Manassas. See Bull Run.
Mason-Dixon Line, 11
McClelland, George B., 32, 42, 119
    Antietam, Battle of, 48
    presidential run, 99
McDowell, Irvin, 24, 25, 26
McLean, Mrs. Eugene, 14
Meade, General George, 70
Military draft, 85, 71–72
Militia Act of 1862, 43
Milliken's Bend, Battle of, 83
Missouri Compromise of 1820, 11
Mosley (slave leader), 16
Mudd, Samuel, 104

N

Nichols, Major George E., 74–75

P

Phillips, Wendell, 40
Pickett, George, 70
Pickett's Charge, 70
Pillow, Fort, 62
Port Hudson, Battle of, 83
Pullman car porters, 111–112

973.7
MCK

McKissack, Pat.

Days of Jubilee :
the end of slavery
in the United States

$16.10

DATE DUE	BORROWER'S NAME	ROOM NO.

973.7
MCK

McKissack, Pat.

Days of Jubilee :
the end of slavery
in the United States

P.S. 309 LIBRARY
794 MONROE ST
BROOKLYN, NY 11221

246414 01610   01069D   006